Statecraft in Symbols

Paul Cheung

Statecraft in Symbols

Policy and the Life of the Chinese Nation

Paul Cheung🆔
Xi'an Jiaotong-Liverpool University
Suzhou, China

ISBN 978-981-19-3318-9   ISBN 978-981-19-3319-6   (eBook)
https://doi.org/10.1007/978-981-19-3319-6

Cover illustration: © Melisa Hasan

This Palgrave Macmillan imprint is published by the registered company Springer Nature Singapore Pte Ltd.
The registered company address is: 152 Beach Road, #21-01/04 Gateway East, Singapore 189721, Singapore

PREFACE

China seems to be on everyone's lips. The China people often talk or think about is both massive and monolithic. These images are also common in what is written about the Chinese government and the Communist Party of China. This book is an examination of how the Chinese state has recently been *presenting* itself through what it *writes* about itself. In the study of public policy reported in the book, there are many signs of the Chinese state presenting itself as anything but monolithic. Similarly, members of the Chinese nation appear in public policy as being highly variegated. Especially for readers interested in policy and polity, what this book offers is an account of the reasons for the Chinese state to go to the lengths as it does in underscoring difference in its own makeup, difference among the citizenry, and difference in the citizenry's interaction with the state.

Suzhou, China   Paul Cheung

CONTENTS

About the Author

Paul Cheung is a sociolinguist based in Xi'an Jiaotong-Liverpool University. His research is centred upon the uses of public-domain communication in dealing with problems of feeding, healing, and housing the population. His work has appeared in periodicals such as *The Lancet Infectious Diseases*, *Medical Journal of Australia* and *Territory, Politics, Governance*. He is also a co-editor of the volume *Suzhou in Transition* (Routledge, 2020).

LIST OF FIGURES

LIST OF TABLES

CHAPTER 1

Divide and Offer

Abstract This chapter introduces the study of statecraft evident in public policy in contemporary China. It begins with the conundrum of rule-by-policy whereby instruments of authority seem to proliferate inexplicably over time. World-historic, action-theoretic, and systems-theoretic paradigmatic perspectives are offered jointly as a way of resolving this conundrum. This leads eventually to the re-working of Karatani Kojin's concept of discursive space into that of the ideological matrix from which ideology in state policy is expected to be re-produced along the dimensions of coherence, progress, and sophistication. The synoptic approach to policy analysis in the present volume is outlined along with the attendant focus upon rhetoric, form, and function. The approach is argued to pave the way for statecraft in China to be shown as much more than what is described proverbially as "divide and conquer".

Keywords Discursive space · Ideological matrix · Public policy · Policy rhetoric · State policy

1.1   POLICY AS SIGNS OF NATIONAL LIFE

Although both of the two proverbial certainties in life are thought to be inescapable, there is one crucial difference between them that often goes unnoticed. Taxes are required by the authorities as a matter of *policy* but death is not. The former are a part of living under rule, while the latter is just a plain fact of life, rule or no rule. Especially if being under rule is really as predictable as the proverb indicates, a number of problems arise. First, no matter which country or region is in question, intuition offers no explanation for the sheer volume and variety of instruments of authority. Secondly, the design of legal, regulatory, and other authoritative instruments is more often than not incomprehensible except to those able to claim expertise over the texts. Thirdly, the impact of policy frequently goes beyond what is stipulated in corresponding expressions of authority. Nevertheless, the cycle of national life continues, and as a part of this, taxes are paid.

This book deals with the conundrum of *rule-by-policy* in contemporary China with a focus on the period spanning 2011 and 2020, a period in which state objectives were said to revolve around modernisation through nation-wide urbanisation. It examines the particularly paradoxical dynamic whereby the citizenry is presented both as homogeneous and heterogeneous in an ever-increasing amount of state policy. As such, this book is a study of policy with respect to the state, society, and relations between the two which one might refer to as politics.

Among the first to theorise connections between modern statecraft, state policy, science, mass education, mass media, and public opinion was Ferdinand Tönnies, who distinguished the law of custom from positive law (1887/2001). Tönnies aligned the former with established tradition and the latter with public policy that evolved with the rise of modern state and society. Whereas custom implied social concord, policy indicated social conflict. Moreover, he pinpointed policy as the site where the state and the people living under its rule are connected, by supposing what today would be called policy *feedback* and consequent changes to policy *settings*. In this sense, policy reflects the workings of the state on the citizenry irrespective of its amount, detail, and efficacy. This kind of symbolic vitality of the state served as the theoretical point of departure for the present study of the life of the Chinese nation through its public policies. Drawing on the work of anthropologists, geographers, linguists, sociologists, policy specialists, political scientists, and others, the present study will hopefully stimulate readers to consider anew how statecraft is sustained in part by symbols.

Despite the conceptualisation of policy as symbolic, there is no intention in this book of uncovering an underlying and unvarying system of signs. Some linguists have provocatively argued that a determinate system of signs might never be found, for the existence of such a system is itself the result of long-standing efforts in symbolic construction (see for example Harris, 2002). Rather than being thought of as pre-determined and systemic, signs are productive in the sense of giving rise to a diversity of forms serving multiple functions. Such potency of signs had already been attested to in a wide range of scholarly works concerning nations large and small, past and present. Aside from Tönnies, who was hinting at the circulation of ideas through written state policy (1887/2001), Marshall Sahlins argued at length for the symbolic constitution of both the value of material goods and the practical interest humans have in such value (1976). Also of consequence here is the example of positive, or written public law, which Niklas Luhmann argued to be a self-regenerating sub-system of communication in a self-reproducing society (Luhmann et al., 1993/2009). Somewhat in concert with Luhmann, Jürgen Habermas developed an extensive account in which positive law, and the policies stemming from it, put in place money and power as mediators of interpersonal and institutional relationships in the course of modernisation (Habermas, 1981a/2005, 1981b/2007; Habermas & Rehg, 1996). Echoing Tönnies' distinction between *Gemeinschaft* from *Gesellschaft*, but examining rural China during the 1930s and 1940s, Fei Xiaotong noted that in the absence of strangers and far from the reaches of the state, written signs formerly had little use in comparison with spoken ones (Fei et al., 1992, pp., (Fei, Hamilton, & Wang, 1992, pp., see also Section 4.3.2).

Policy, as written signs, is assumed to be an instrument of the state whose usefulness lies in its potential to produce, and reproduce, variation. On the basis of this point of departure, the notion of universal policy would be oxymoronic. In the realm of statecraft, variability is one of the most significant and salient features of policy. As noted in previous work on contemporary non-Chinese states, differences within the populace were constructed to render some segments as more deserving of policy support than other segments, for instance with respect to social welfare (for a review, see Ingram et al., 2007). Any constructed difference, not being inherent, calls into question the social and political ideals encapsulated in terms such as "belonging", "equality", and "freedom". The converse, namely the symbolic rendering of difference into similarity has received considerably less attention among scholars. If written signs are as contingent in their operation as some scholars insist, it would be important to examine construction of both similarity as well as difference. As shall be shown throughout this book, the contingently similar is not necessarily separate from the contingently different in the workings of the Chinese state if state policy is considered in symbolic terms.

Several inter-related policy domains were included in the present study of state policy in contemporary China, namely, household registration, public service entitlements, language use, and natural disaster management. These policy domains are among those which pertain to the indeterminate relationship between people and the land they reside upon, a relationship that is mediated by geographical variation across the Chinese nation. Policies in these domains address state proscriptions and provisions, mostly to do with the conditions under which residency occurs, among a sizeable population within a culturally, economically, linguistically, and socially diverse territory. As such, these policies can be expected as sites where any contradiction between the state as *arbiter* and the state as *leveller* is symbolically operated on. Further, by reading policies across domains synoptically, the ways in which state policy reproduces itself could be identified.

The next section of the introduction provides an orientation to the array of theoretical problems arising from the conundrum of rule-by-policy with reference to three paradigms: the world-historic, the action-theoretic, and the systems-theoretic. Upon the theoretical bases associated with these paradigms, an overview is then offered of the major conceptual terms of reference to be employed in the present study of Chinese state policy. This will be followed by a brief overview of analytical uses of such conceptual terms. The introduction ends with an outline of subsequent analytical chapters and the postscript.

1.2   THEORISING POLICY AS STATECRAFT

1.2.1   Policy as Invariably Varied

If statecraft were solely political profiteering at any cost, state policy should be straightforwardly standard. Instead of persistently constructing difference or similarity, policy merely needs to apply largely the same measure uniformly, subject only to similarly uniform adjustments in the face of circumstantial threats. Whether changing over time or not, policy would be largely undifferentiated across the state in such a hypothetical scenario. Political thought, however, would have policy as a state instrument that not only differentiates, but is itself highly differentiated within the jurisdiction of the state. Not long after Tönnies offered his own account of society's emergence on the basis of positive law (Tönnies, 1887/2001), he brought to readers a new compilation of the English-language works of Thomas Hobbes. In this collection (1889/1928), which includes the 1650 treatises *The Fundamental Elements of Policy*[1] and *The Elements of Law, Moral and Politic*,[2] Hobbes made a clear distinction between the personal sovereign and all other human entities. Rule by the sovereign was held by Hobbes to be the condition for "common peace, defence and benefit" among subjects (p. 81). By extension, the hierarchical relationship forming the basis of the body politic was reproduced downwards as corporations, each of which was "a subordinate union of certain men, for certain common actions to be done by those men for some common benefit of theirs, or of the whole city" (ibid.). Although according to Hobbes, fear of rulers large and small was the common basis of subordination, subjects had varying interests from each other. The very purpose of civil law, the political extension of natural law in Hobbes' view, was to bring diverse interests under the common rule of the sovereign, and not to unify interests *per se*. Further, in the more frequently cited *Leviathan*, civil law was such for delineating "what is contrary, and what is not contrary to the Rule" (1651, p. 117). Hobbes had no problem in accommodating the positive law of conquered lands, which unlike natural law was by definition not universal. Importantly, he also referred to the distinction between fundamental civil law and non-fundamental civil law. Non-fundamental civil law was directed at resolving differences between subjects and as such could be annulled without dismembering the body politic. Based on fear of the ruler and varying interests then, civil law, as positive law, would serve the function of ordering national life at all levels.

Under different and disconnected historical circumstances was an apologist for the ruler whose political thought coincided with Hobbes'

---

[1] With the short title of *Human Nature*.

[2] With the short title of *De Corpore Politico*.

on many crucial points. Living in the Warring States period (453–221 B.C.E.), Shang Yang was a leading proponent of the kind of expansionism which contributed to the feudal state of Qin[3] being enlarged into a continental empire by the same title. Surviving to this day in a collection known as *Shang Jun Shu* (商君书,1928, 2017),[4] proposals made by Shang Yang and followers revolved around the consolidation of power and resources by the state. As with Hobbes, Shang Yang sought to empower the ruler by means of positive law, through which the ruler's role would be enshrined while simultaneously undermining the threat posed by aristocrats. As part of the securing of patronage, both figures exempted rulers from proscriptions against inherited privilege, and justified policy proposals on the basis of an irrevocably negative portrayal of human nature. The pair was adamant that laws be recorded not for its own sake, but in order to facilitate promulgation and legitimise punishments. And both presented peace as the main reward for being under rule. Moreover, Shang Yang went further than Hobbes in drawing out the implications of the purportedly inborn selfishness of subjects, suggesting for instance that this vulnerability be exploited through the creation of dissimilar interests among state functionaries (Yang, 2017, p. 238)[5]:

> *Therefore, the regulations of the ordered states are such that the people cannot escape punishment, just as whatever the eye has seen cannot escape one's mind. Yet nowadays in disordered states this is not so: they rely on manifold officials and numerous clerks. Yet though the clerks are numerous, their essence is the same: and those whose essence is the same cannot [supervise] each other. Therefore, the former kings safeguarded themselves by making [the officials'] benefits different and disadvantages unequal.*

In his brand of statecraft, Shang Yang expounded considerably more on incentive schemes for different parts of the populace than Hobbes ever did through his notion of corporations. Shang Yang's proposals contrived incentives and disincentives thought to be conducive to the chief political imperative of the time: lasting victory at a time of inter-state conflict.

---

[3] Covering mainly parts of present-day Shaanxi Province in China.

[4] Also known as *Shangzi* (商子, shāngzǐ).

[5] Translated by Yuri Pines from the following: 故治國之制, 民不得避罪, 如目不能以所見遁心。今亂國不然, 恃多官眾吏。吏雖眾, 事同體一也。夫事同體一者, 相監不可。且夫利異而害不同者, 先王所以為保也。

This imperative meant among other things tying the populace to the land in order to add to granaries, or else committing the populace to territorial expansion, all the while encouraging inbound migration from other states and discouraging trade in goods. Beyond *Shang Jun Shu*, it was recorded for example that Shang Yang tried to double the tax burden upon undivided households with two or more adult male offspring (refer to notes in Shang Yang, 1928, Shang Yang, 2017). Across what would be called different policy domains today then, Shang Yang devised a rather intricate system of mutually reinforcing measures with a view of perpetuating orderly rule for the long term. These measures would not have been possible by homogenising the entire populace (Handelman, 1995). Instead, for posterity, Shang Yang advocated the cross-classification of the populace according to multiple criteria so that in principle, rewards and sanctions were issued at the state's own discretion. Shang Yang displayed in his thought the kind of instrumentalism that was much more than political expediency aimed at short-term gain, and certainly not one that was devoid of a larger worldview (see the commentary by Jan Duyvendak in Shang Yang, 1928). Inasmuch Shang Yang construed human nature negatively in justification of human rule positively, he was also reconfiguring the constellation of relations within the cosmology prevailing in his time (Handelman, 1995). Likewise, Hobbes was in effect rewriting theology as it was known to his own contemporaries. With the examples of Hobbes and Shang Yang in mind, invariably varied state policy could be more usefully theorised as being functionalist (cf. Fei et al., 1992) in orientation rather than realist (cf. Fischer, 2012). In other words, having state policy invariably vary was for these figures the means of intentionally sustaining rule by the few by governing relations among the multitude in a discretionary manner.

1.2.2   China as a Policy-Issuing Entity

Shang Yang and Hobbes were only two of many notable figures in political thought. Despite the traces each left, by no means was either the sole representative in any way of the East or the West. Nonetheless, the coincidences in their thought are theoretically germane to this book on contemporary state policy in China. First, in different parts of the world and at different times state policy could actually serve similar political functions if not the same political function. The political function of state policy at a particular juncture may not be unique to China or to other political entities throughout history. Secondly, state policy may follow the same overall tendency of dividing and ruling in spite of differences in political form taken by states. If so, the Chinese state is theoretically comparable to other states without any requirement for states to be identical in form. Thirdly, state policies in different policy domains could be connected by the propensity of policy's overall political function and not necessarily by virtue of their provenance. Hence despite the different circumstances leading to their launch, and their ostensibly different objectives, state policies in different domains in China are also theoretically comparable without being identical to each other. Fourth, state policy is not simply the prerogative of those topping the political hierarchy; the agency of state actors lower down also deserves attention. Theoretically, this implies comparison of policy made by different kinds and levels of state organs of China. Lastly, policy needs to be considered not only within the boundaries of the issuing state, but that of the states it interacts with also. Persistent focus upon Chinese state policy would nonetheless require the consideration of geopolitics but not necessarily the kind that turns the present study into a comparative one.

The above caveats require theorising of statecraft in contemporary China that recognises domestic issues as geopolitical ones. How then is China to be theorised as a policy-issuing entity that is also part of the geopolitical order? Also in this regard Tönnies provided a point of departure for this seemingly simple problem. Tönnies, who was ambivalent about the distinction of Gesellschaft from the state, still saw both as operating within the world market (Tönnies, 1887/2001), and speculated on the replacements of Gesellschaft, which supposedly superseded Gemeinschaft. One possibility Tönnies made passing reference to was the "world state" (p. 238), which assumed the international division of labour as well as trade between constituent states. Tönnies' world state mirrors Hobbes' sovereign polity in that it is a union with constituent units, albeit on a global scale. However, the two envisaged relations between nations differently. For Hobbes, the natural tendency towards self-preservation which underlies relations between individuals would be extended on the global scale to shape relations between nations (see Chapter 10 of Part II of Hobbes & Tönnies, 1889/1928). In contrast, Tönnies saw these relations to be regulated by forces of demand and supply in the world market, with little elaboration, other than the condition of each constituent state co-existing with their own capitalists. Significantly, in an addendum made in 1922 Tönnies appeared less optimistic, and more like Hobbes, when he referred to the degeneration of the Gesellschaft based on "world capitalism" (p. 210). The addendum was included, according to Tönnies, in response to readers' attempts to find hope in the antecedent formation of Gemeinschaft, and its contrasts to Gesellschaft. Not explicitly addressed by Tönnies were the alignment if any of non-European political entities with Gesellschaft and the prospect of Gesellschaft reverting into Gemeinschaft anywhere in the world. Importantly, both of these problems had long been prefigured in *Shang Jun Shu* all the way back in the Fourth Century B.C.E. without China's participation in any global capitalist order until much later in history.

Instead of "world capitalism", Immanuel Wallerstein referred to the "capitalist world-system", "modern world-system", or "modern world-economy", which in his lengthy study was the culmination of centuries of struggle for supremacy within Europe (Wallerstein, 2011a, 2011b, 2011c, 2011d). Crucially, these struggles did not proceed in a linear fashion, but through cycles of economic contraction, and less frequently, rise of a new international hegemon. In Wallerstein's analysis, hegemony in such a system was achieved by the United Provinces[6] in the seventeenth century, and later by Great Britain in the eighteenth century and nineteenth century. Wallerstein argued that one of the most important consequences of the quest for European hegemony was the brand of political thought which he labelled "centrist liberalism". Centrist liberalism was held by Wallerstein to be the exemplar of geopolitical culture from the eighteenth century onward, even when it appeared in the guise of conservatism and socialism. Although unlike in earlier times, hegemony was on a much larger scale, all three brands of political thought shared the state-consolidating tendency of fifteenth century absolutism, which was manifest in form of monarchy. Monarchy had earlier come under absolutism through a combination of "bureaucratization, monopolization of force, creation of legitimacy, and homogenization of the subject population" (Wallerstein, 2011d, p. 136). In contrast with absolutism, however, on eighteenth-century political thought a premium was placed upon heterogeneity, with the purpose of supporting the creation of surplus value and accumulation of capital. Heterogeneity was, in Wallerstein's account, projected not only upon global geography in the development of the modern world-system, but also on domestic geography, expanding

---

[6] Present-day Netherlands.

the scope within which differentials could be defined. Human capital was likewise particularised to facilitate its deployment for accumulation, setting the historical stage for the ancient Greek notions of citizenship and equality among individual citizens to be appropriated. The citizen of the modern world-system, Wallerstein observed, was a contradiction resulting from the creation of difference despite the promise of sameness, a contradiction for which centrist liberalism was tailored specifically to resolve (2011a, p. 156):

> *The great socially unifying concept of the citizen thus led to the formalization of multiple cross-cutting binary categories and the binary tension of political life -- the split between right and left...that centrist liberalism would devote all its efforts to rendering meaningless.*

Wallerstein's diagnosis of the malaise of the modern world, at least the "capitalist" portion of it, was one afflicted by contrived distinctions between people, places, and things. Whatever the merits of his argumentation, or lack of, there are again coincidences between his account of world history leading to the present time and the earlier political thought of Shang Yang and Hobbes. That is, under a range of geopolitical circumstances featuring fierce inter-state competition on a large scale, variation in state policy within, and in polity between national jurisdictions, was conducive to the consolidation of state power. Conversely, it is theoretically possible that under a different set of circumstances, state policy would have favoured wholesale homogenisation, and still other circumstances, a mixture of heterogenisation with homogenisation. The variability of state policy is therefore not necessarily or fully contingent on state form, irrespective of whether state form is identified as feudal, imperial, liberal, conservative, or socialist. In a broadly world-historic paradigm then, neither would overall state policy orientation in respect of variability bear a deterministic relationship with designations such as "authoritarian" or "free", "communist" or "democratic", "emerging" or "established". As such, China as a policy-issuing entity and its membership in the modern world-system require study on its own terms as opposed with being carried out presumptively on the basis of these often polemical dichotomies.

1.2.3   China as Part of the Modern World-System

To the extent that the modern world-system is theoretically meaningful, a problem that stems from its use in the study of contemporary Chinese state policy would be the variability of geopolitical order itself, and changes to China as a policy-issuing entity in a different order. In Shang Yang, as in Hobbes; for Tönnies, and for Wallerstein, the consolidation of state power meant the enlargement of the scale of politics. What alternatives are there then to the modern world-system, and to the seemingly modern world economy? Wallerstein has yet to publish the next instalment of his account, intended to address further developments of the modern world-system beyond the year 1914. And clearly, Tönnies' world state has not yet come to pass.

Within a world-historic paradigm, the scale of politics and number of geopolitical orders are concerns not only in relation to the future, but the present and past as well. In this respect, Karatani Kojin offered much by way of further theoretical developments to those produced by Wallerstein and Tönnies. For Karatani, geopolitical order had in earlier times been defined by "World Empire" and "Mini-world System" (Karatani, 2010/2014, p. 28; 2012/2017, p. 138). Drawing on his own reading of Immanuel Kant and Karl Marx, Karatani theorised the "World Republic" as a geopolitical order which could replace the modern "World Economy" in the sense intended by Wallerstein, but extended to cover the period after 1914. Karatani regarded each change of order as involving the subsuming of other orders, and as an ultimately futile way of reverting to the most primal mode of exchange, or what he referred to as "gift and countergift" (Karatani, 2010/2014, p. 5; 2012/2017, p. 135). Accordingly, the dominant mode of exchange for each geopolitical order could be schematically represented in Fig. 1.1.

In Karatani's conceptualisation, the mini-world-system is in effect the ancient world-system in which rule was exercised over small domains, and in which life was characterised by a nomadic or tribal existence devoid of material accumulation or long-term settlement. Politics in this era was therefore limited in geographical scale. World empires subsequently emerged through the partial transcendence above, and also the partial transformation of, these local domains. Despite not being entirely erased in the course of such *geopolitical sublation*, reciprocity was supposedly overtaken by plunder and redistribution as the dominant mode of exchange. And after replacing one another, world empires disintegrated,

B: plunder and redistribution	A: gift and countergift
World Empire	Mini-world System
C: commodity exchange	D: reversion to reciprocity
World Economy	World Republic
(The modern world system)	

Fig. 1.1 Dominant mode of exchange in each geopolitical order (Adapted from Karatani, 2008, 2010/2014, 2012/2017)

followed by the rise of the modern world-system for which Wallerstein provided a European account. For his part, Karatani saw the modern world-system as resulting from the sublation of local domains and former empires. This also meant commodification overtaking reciprocity and redistribution as the main mode of exchange. Karatani noted that dissatisfaction with the inequality inherent in the commodification of labour and land would lead to ineffectual attempts at reforming the order of world capitalism, only for the order to remain largely unchanged. To borrow terms again from Tönnies, Karatani did not regard the prospect of Gesellschaft (cf. world economy) reverting into Gemeinschaft (cf. ancient world-system) to be likely. Instead, if there is to be a different era, it would result from the further sublation of nation-states in the modern world-system into a world republic.

Interestingly, in his own reading, Karatani (e.g. 2008, 2014) cast the world republic, the back translation from "Völkerbund" ('federation of nations', see Kant, 2007, p. 114) as one example of what Kant referred to as the "regulative principle of reason" (Kant, 1781/1988, p. 544) or the "regulative use of the ideas and pure reason" (Kant, 1781/1988, p. 590). The appeal to the convoluted argumentation in Kant's *Critique of Pure Reason* was Karatani's way of underscoring the regulative or guiding property of the concept of Völkerbund rather than the predictive certainty of the same. As Kant himself put it in a manner which reminds one of Hobbes, Völkerbund's emergence was not likely either due to the sublation of self-preserving instincts all the way up to inter-state level (Kant, 2007, p. 116):

> As long, however, as states apply all their powers to their vain and violent aims of expansion and thus ceaselessly constrain the slow endeavor of the inner formation of their citizens' mode of thought, also withdrawing with this aim all support from it, nothing of this kind is to be expected, because it would require a long inner labor of every commonwealth for the education of its citizens. But everything good that is not grafted onto a morally good disposition, is nothing but mere semblance and glittering misery. In this condition humankind will remain until, in the way I have said, it will labor its way out of the chaotic condition of the present relations between states.

Closely connected to geopolitical sublation is Karatani's emphasis upon repetition in history. In his analysis, sublation implied the retaining of both geopolitical forms and modes of exchange from the past, even as they appeared to be subsumed under the new. What Karatani meant by *hanpuku*,[7] translated into English as repetition, is not the complete replication of circumstances over time and across locations (Karatani & Lippit, 2004/2004). Rather than being a duplicate of the past, repetition is a matter of correspondence, a relation of both similarity and difference. For greater clarity, these correspondences will be referred to henceforth as *recursions*. Examples of recursion that Karatani gave included the rise once more of China, India, and Russia in the new millennium. Without the concept of recursion, any similarity between China in any two given historical periods may be seen as a matter of cyclical return at the cost of ignoring the differences. Conversely, any difference in two periods may be understood as part of a linear trend, but only if recursions are ignored. The emphasis on both sublation and recursion led Karatani to continue analysing the development of world capitalism beyond 1914, the time during which he saw the United States as achieving global hegemony. The present study can be seen as an addition to this effort through its focus upon China in the prevailing and yet mutating geopolitical order.

---

[7] That is, 反復 (はんぷく).

The world-historic contentions put forward by Tönnies, Wallerstein, and Karatani allow China in the years between 2011 and 2020 to be identified geopolitically as a competitive participant in the world economy, specifically in the sense of a policy-issuing entity in which the commodification of labour and land dominated over reciprocity and redistribution as the mode of exchange domestically. Expressed differently, despite whatever differences in polity between China and its main competitor the United States, geopolitically the two entities are members of the same modern world-system in many respects, not the least of which is the heavy reliance of each on its own citizens' commodified labour and land. What the state offers to the citizenry in return varies from policy domain to policy domain, and within each, individually, not to mention other conceivable permutations. Furthermore, together with any apparent change, rule-by-policy is partially replicated from the past. In respect of China, the above contentions will be examined in detail in the remainder of the present volume with reference also to insights taken from action-theoretic and systems theoretic paradigms.

1.2.4   China as Active Constituent Systems

Within the world-historic paradigm introduced thus far, contemporary Chinese state policy is supposed to be invariably variable, much like that of other major players in the modern world-system. What could be lacking in such a paradigm for the study of ostensibly domestic policy is theorisation of the state as conceptually distinct from its relations with other states. When conceived of as a system, or as constituent systems, an additional aspect becomes salient in the analysis of state policy. In this regard, two paradigms complementary to the world-historic one are particularly relevant to the present study of statecraft in symbols: the action-theoretic and the systems-theoretic. Exemplary of the systems-theoretic is Luhmann through his work on legal theory and the sociology of law, especially *Law as a Social System* (Luhmann et al., 1993/2009), and also Habermas, who in addition brought to bear the action-theoretic influence of Talcott Parsons[8] on his own formulation of state-society relations under late capitalism. Habermas' extensive oeuvre culminated in *The*

---

[8] See for instance Parsons, T., & Shils, E. A. (Eds.). (1951/1962). *Toward a General Theory of Action*. Cambridge: Harvard.

Theory of Communicative Action (1981a/2005, 1981b/2007), in which the impact of speech act theory[9] is also evident.

Both Habermas and Luhmann conceptualised society and analysed it in terms of systems and sub-systems.[10] They differ in how these constituent elements of society were conceptualised in relation to each other. For Habermas, constituent elements were "action systems" in the sense that they exert influences upon each other, equally or otherwise. Hence the variety of systems and sub-systems were open to rather than being closed off from each other. Habermas distinguished two main action systems in operation in society: "lifeworld" and "system". *Lifeworld*, typified by family and community, is meant to be oriented to the primal mode of social existence and characterised by linguistically negotiated reciprocity. In contrast, *system*, chiefly made up of state administration and the monetary economy, is putatively founded upon institutionalisation and oriented towards instrumental gain for some but not for all. Habermas argued that since early capitalism, lifeworld has been colonised by system through positive law, the kind based less on established custom but more on evolving convention, again to borrow terms used by Tönnies. Through positive law, system formally organises lifeworld, thereby instrumentalising or rationalising it. Crucially for the present study, Habermas also attributed to system the functionalist orientation towards self-perpetuation and the tendency to be increasingly "decoupled" from the communicative rationality of lifeworld. Despite being overwhelmed by system, lifeworld is far from erased from society. Instead, the communicatively structured interaction of lifeworld takes on more and more of the purposive rationality of system. As such, incursion of system into lifeworld is not only administrative, but also ideological. Habermas tried to demonstrate the incursion of system into lifeworld through increasing involvement by system in such formerly private matters as ageing, childrearing, education, and health (1981b/2007, see especially page 361 and onward).

[9] See for example Searle, J. R. (1969). *Speech Acts: An essay in the philosophy of language.* London: Cambridge University Press.

[10] Despite the fact that both Habermas and Luhmann have a penchant for interchangeably using "system" with "sub-system", the point of interest is the analytical divisibility of Gesellschaft in the dictionary sense into constituent entities. The divisions, being analytical, are necessary arbitrary as opposed to absolute.

Habermas regarded "bureaucratic-socialist societies" under one-party rule with state monopolisation of most means of production as having taken the developmental path that branched off after the rise of capitalism. He asserted that bureaucratic-socialist societies, the defining criteria for which contemporary China would seem to meet, are those where life-world comes under the influence of system in a different way as ostensibly capitalist societies (Habermas, 1981b/2007, p. 386):

> But instead of the reification of communicative relations we find the sham-ming of communicative relations in bureaucratically desiccated, forcibly "humanized" domains of pseudopolitical intercourse in an overextended and administered public sphere. This pseudopoliticization is symmetrical to reifying privatization in certain respects. The lifeworld is not directly assimi-lated to the system, that is, to legally regulated, formally organized domains of action; rather, systemically self-sufficient organizations are actively put back into a simulated horizon of the lifeworld. While the system is draped out as the lifeworld, the lifeworld is absorbed by the system.

Some of Habermas' assertions in relation to bureaucratic-socialist societies, like the world-historic contentions laid out above, will be examined in the analytical treatment of contemporary Chinese state policy in this book. Suffice to indicate at this point that what the world-historic paradigm adds to the action-theoretic paradigm is a more nuanced inter-pretation of the variability of world capitalism, thereby minimising the risk of obscuring features of the Chinese state as a member of the modern world-system. Similarly, the action-theoretic paradigm will be adopted in the present study to avoid some of the excesses of the systems-theoretic paradigm as exemplified by Luhmann. In turn, the systems-theoretic will be used in a way complementary to the world-historic and action-theoretic.

Unlike Habermas, Luhmann was less concerned with the interac-tion between systems and sub-systems, and more with the autonomy of law. Contrasting law with politics and constituent elements of the state, Luhmann was adamant about the properties which make the former autonomous in spite of otherwise being inter-dependent with respect to the latter (Luhmann et al., 1993/2009). Specifically, Luhmann saw the legal system as self-describing, self-distinguishing, self-referring and above all, as a result, self-sustaining. These properties of law are also what contributes to the *autopoiesis* or self-reproduction of society. In this sense, the legal system is operatively closed off from the political system as it endlessly determines the legality of its objects. Luhmann did not claim absolute closure, only that in law's operation, as a kind of sub-system of societal communication, it acts as if it is autonomous. Yet law is supposed to be "cognitively open" in the sense of the capacity to respond to contingencies beyond the system, and without itself being transformed fundamentally in the process. The twin concepts of *operational closure* and *cognitive openness* harmonise Luhmann's theoretical claims about law's self-reproduction on the one hand, and about law's self-correction on the other. Overall, Luhmann's account as a social system can be treated as a functionalist account of rule.

Although Luhmann also characterised the political system as operationally closed, he was sufficiently preoccupied with arguing the case for systemic autonomy not to elaborate on the mutual influences of systems. The latter is a strength of Habermas' emphasis upon the actions of one system upon another system. And despite being aware of Habermas' concept of lifeworld, Luhmann was silent on the communication stemming from it and law's influences on it. Nonetheless, for the purposes of the present study Luhmann's contributions to systems-theoretic paradigm are additional to Habermas' and advantageous in a number of ways. First, Luhmann, more directly than Habermas, appears to offer a theoretical solution to the conundrum of symbolic excess in law, especially law within any given area. Secondly, Luhmann more prominently accounts for the discursive manifestations of rule, albeit only the part of positive law that is legislation, and not the part that is public policy. Thirdly, in casting law as invariably varied, Luhmann's concepts are paradigmatically compatible with concerns in this book over whether in contemporary public policy in China one can identify instrumental, and more precisely, functionalist rationality. Lastly, but not least, the self-reproduction of law, in being non-duplicative, makes positive law conceptually consistent with the world-historic notion of recursion of geopolitical order and of modes of exchange. Indeed, as shall be demonstrated later in this book, positive law, inclusive of its public policy component, embodies the symbolic loci, means, and processes for such recursion.

Below the main conceptual terms of reference for the present study are defined within the world-historic, action-theoretic, and systems-theoretic paradigms introduced above. Where applicable, contrasting conceptualisations arising from differences in paradigmatic reasoning are highlighted.

1.3   Conceptualising Chinese State Policy

1.3.1   Statehood, the Citizenry and Nationhood

The present study is one of statecraft as evidenced in contemporary policy of the Chinese state, especially in the domains of household registration, public service entitlements, language use, and natural disaster management. As such, it is a study of the state and how it relates to society, and vice versa, through policy.

In respect of the state as a unit of analysis, complete identification with society would be problematic, as already noted in Habermas' response to Luhmann's version of systems-theory. Equally, however, the state needs to be conceptualised as more than the administrative action system differentiated by the steering medium of power as Habermas preferred to. The sense of a state as an over-arching presence among others in the global scene, however intangible such a presence might be, remains a very useful insight borrowed from the world-historic paradigm. Such a sense does not necessarily commit one to the study of domestic policy primarily as international policy, or to the comparison of policy between states, but draws attention to that part of society that is not the state. As a concept, *statehood* delineates rule from other aspects of society, and implies an ineluctable political kinship centred on the state (cf. Sahlins, 2008). The resulting collective, as noted by Wallerstein, is one built on different kinds and degrees of exclusion, despite the symbolic construction of inclusion in the term "*the citizenry*" (Wallerstein, 2011a). Given this kind of inter-connection of the ruler and the ruled then, *nationhood* is conceptualised as the embodiment of all of the following: the state, the citizenry, and relations between them. Once again, rather than entirely being predictable, statehood, citizenship, and nationhood are expected to show considerable variability when their symbolic construction in policy comes under analysis.

1.3.2   Policy and Policy Density

Unless as otherwise indicated, policy refers to *state policy* in the present study. Following Tönnies (1887/2001), policy is treated as the superordinate category inclusive of both legal and non-legal policy, and the paradigmatic equivalent to positive law but not natural law. The overall imperative of policy is preservation of the state and the administration of populace in service of this objective. Although policy pertains to the public in this administrative sense, is not necessarily created with the consent of members of the public, or for their consumption. Interest in, and knowledge of, and contribution to policy by the public are possible but not a given.

As interface between the state and the citizenry, but not necessarily that between system and lifeworld, policy takes a variety of enacted, encoded, or other symbolic forms. These forms are produced through legislative or other means. Non-legal policy, commonly referred to as *public policy*, is the main object of the present study. Where relevant, legal policy will also be subjected to analysis. Whereas the workings of the law as a symbolic maker of state and society have attracted much attention in among legal sociologists (e.g. Perez & Teubner, 2006; Teubner, 1987), the same could not be said about non-legal, or public policy. Habermas labelled the particular kind of incursion of system into lifeworld through households through positive law in democratic welfare states as "jurid-ification" (1981b/2007, p. 357). Through "juridification", particular circumstances of facing the elderly, the young, and the unwell are deemed to call for public support, effectively excluding those in other circumstances. Although no equivalent term for the expansion of policy was offered, Habermas was very close to elaborating on the consequences of the policy equivalent of "juridification", which shall be referred to henceforth as "policification". He nonetheless provided the observation that whatever legally guaranteed welfare for the citizenry in defined social situations may remain unrealised during bureaucratic implementation of the relevant laws. As the concepts of modes of exchange and world capitalism, both taken from the world-historic paradigm, support a less categorical distinction between bureaucratic-socialist societies and democratic welfare states, juridification and policification are contentions deserving of serious consideration in contemporary China. It is worth reiterating how even within an action-theoretic paradigm Habermas regarded bureaucratic-socialist societies as those that were once on the same developmental path as those states that are now ostensibly capitalist in orientation (see Sect. 1.2.4). The systems-theoretic and communicative action-theoretic insights highlighted thus far suggest strongly a pragmatic as opposed to formalist conceptualisation of policy. By relying on these insights, policy is understood in this book as communication at the societal level whose form, function, outcome, significance, and legacy are as variable as the state and non-state actors involved in the process.

For their part, policy specialists, who mostly do not draw on insights from world-historic, action-theoretic, and systems-theoretic paradigms, have independently come to empirical observations compatible with Habermas' concept of juridification. From non-paradigmatic perspectives, these specialists have written extensively on such dysfunctional phenomena as policy layering (e.g. Thelen, 2004), policy drift (e.g. Hacker, 2004), policy accumulation (e.g. Adam et al., 2019), and policy mix (e.g. Howlett & Rayner, 2013). Significantly, such research into policy in contemporary states also provides support to Luhmann's concept of autopoiesis as it is extended to public policy. Existing theoretical and empirical work underscores the tendency for policy to expand in scope and growth in complexity over time without necessarily being accompanied by commensurate enhancement in domain-specific efficacy. In the present study, such general increase in *policy density* is nonetheless expected to work, intentionally or incidentally, in favour of state consolidation under world capitalism.

1.3.3   Policy in Discursive Space

Habermas' diagnosis of the malaise of late capitalism focused on the actions of the administrative system and economic system on lifeworld. The only refinement he offered to the conceptualisation of positive law as the interface between system and lifeworld was the characterisation of law as an extension of the steering medium of power (see for example Habermas, 1981b/2007, pp. 372–373). In other words, for Habermas, the medium of law, together with the medium of power, tend to have the effect of replacing, however incompletely, the rationality underlying human communication, reciprocity, with that of the preservation of the status quo. From the latter stem other, more specific imperatives of system. Given that the medium of law is discursive, such imperatives can potentially be discerned as symbolic constructions of values. As with the lack of elaboration upon public policy as a steering medium, few details were available on systemic imperatives other than their theoretical existence. Similarly, Luhmann did not fully address external drivers of change to the legal system due to his emphasis upon law's own self-reproducing tendencies. How the self-reproduction of the law may lead to the reformulation of values in other systems of societal communication, and vice versa, was not a problem he dealt with (Luhmann et al., 1993/2009).

Additional conceptual moves are therefore necessary in investigating the ideology by which policy steers life under rule.

It was Tönnies who noted at the end of the nineteenth century that changes to policy were subject in part to public opinion, which in turn was informed by science and education via mass media (Tönnies,, 1887/2001). As if to add to Tönnies' implicitly stated notion of policy feedback, Wallerstein made a compelling argument for centrist liberalism as the very basis of modern social sciences and their supposed Eurocentric tendencies (Wallerstein, 2011a). Conceptually, writers like Tönnies and Wallerstein had effectively opened up the possibility of public opinion being gradually made to share ideals comparable to, or at least compatible with, the imperatives of the state as world capitalism extended its geographical reach. Conversely, one could thereby extend Habermas by raising the possibility of system passing its imperatives off as values acceptable to lifeworld in addition to undermining the reciprocally communicative structure of lifeworld. If so, policy would not so much be an instrument of unidirectional force as one of subtle co-optation.

Paradigmatically then, political imperatives of the state are manifest in policy, and are simultaneously reflected imperfectly in ideals as found in other systems of societal communication such as mass media. Through his analysis of societal communication in Meiji, Taisho, and Showa Japan (i.e. Japan during the years spanning 1868 and 1989), Karatani identified continua along which ideals could be plotted. The resulting conceptual device, *discursive space* (Karatani & Lippit, 2004/2012), was used to chart prominent writers and other figures of different political persuasions, and where applicable, changes in how they envisioned the ideal Japanese nation. The modern Japanese nation-state had only emerged late in the nineteenth century, when power was wrested from the military government under the Shogun and from various provincial *daimyo* or samurai feudal lords who formed unstable alliances with the Shogun. Geopolitically, the feudal domains making up Japan were variously embroiled with Western powers which sought to exert control over the entire archipelago. These developments set the scene for debates over what the nation, which was eventually unified under the symbolic authority of a constitutional monarch, actually meant. Was it a national community sustained by the centralisation of political power? Further, was it a nation ready to embark on a new path to greatness, a path exemplified by the course taken by those Western powers fuelled by colonial ambitions? Karatani attempted to capture the possible responses to these

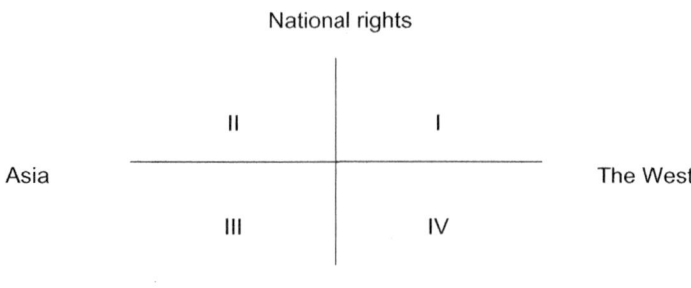

Fig. 1.2 The discursive space of modern Japan (Adapted from Karatani & Lippit, 2004/2012. History and Repetition. Columbia University Press, p. 56

questions by assigning the following poles to two intersecting continua: national rights—popular rights and Asia—the West, as shown in Fig. 1.2.

Along the national rights—popular rights continuum Karatani located the ideals associated with centralisation and decentralisation. Similarly, ideals concerning Japan's developmental path were placed on the Asia—the West continuum. The contrast between Asia and the West was crucial not only due to the catalytic effects of colonial ambitions displayed towards Japan by distant foreign powers, but also to the long-standing influence of China during its imperial epoch. As only one example of an ideal on the latter continuum, Karatani noted the rather starkly stated doctrine of "abandoning Asia for Europe"[11] that was advanced by Fukuzawa Yukichi in 1885 (see Karatani & Lippit, 2004/2012, pp. 64–65). According to this doctrine, Japan ought to leave behind the imported heritage of Confucianism and embrace the liberal ideals consistent with a state featuring a bourgeois class.

By means of the discursive space then, Karatani attempted to demonstrate the increasingly greater emphasis upon both national rights and Asia in societal communication in Japan since the late nineteenth century. This move within the discursive space was termed "interiority" (Karatani, 1993/1998, pp. 11–75). In turn, he theorised *interiority* to be a process which increasingly privileged inward-looking self-consciousness against a

---

[11] That is, 脱亜入欧 (だつあにゅうおう, datsu-a-ny-uo).

hitherto imperceptible geopolitical scenery characterised by the world economy. As Wallerstein has argued, the world economy underlying the capitalist world-system would not have come into existence without the ideological support of contrived distinctions and ideological structures in which such distinctions are privileged. Conceptually, this means that the discursive space could be employed in two ways not previously attempted: to locate within it the kind of societal communication defined as policy, and to do so for other national entities under the influence of, and sublated into, the modern world-system. The approach to Chinese state policy in this book retains Karatani's emphasis upon the criss-crossing of ideals and changes to ideals over time, but reconceptualises the continua along which they can be identified for greater consistency with the world-historic paradigm. Hence national integration replaces national rights on one end of the first continuum. The lack of national integration, or fragmentation, replaces popular rights on the other end of the same continuum. Along the second continuum, the West is replaced with advancement and Asia with regress. Moreover, as different strands of political thought and practice seem to have converged on the same emphasis upon differentiation, a third continuum is required. At one end of the additional continuum is diversity, and on the other, uniformity. Respectively, the three continua relate to the coherence of the nation-state, its progress towards a desirable end, and the sophistication which is attributed to diversity. Given the employment of systems-theoretic and communicative action-theoretic insights together with the world-historic, it would be necessary to highlight the reproductive capacity of the above ideals. Therefore, instead of a two-dimensional discursive space, an ideological matrix with three dimensions is suggested as a heuristic in upcoming analyses of contemporary Chinese state policy. This ideological matrix is presented in Fig. 1.3.

Especially from a world-historic perspective, it is in an ideological matrix such as the one illustrated in Fig. 1.3 that many ideals of statehood, the citizenry and nationhood are conceived. In being multidimensional, these ideals are expected to both complement and contradict each other. The manner in which and extent to which these ideals correspond to the imperatives of the state will be explored analytically in subsequent chapters. The conceptual point of departure related to the employment of the ideological matrix was simply that in policy, state imperatives may somehow have been reproduced, however partially, with ideals enjoying currency in civil society.

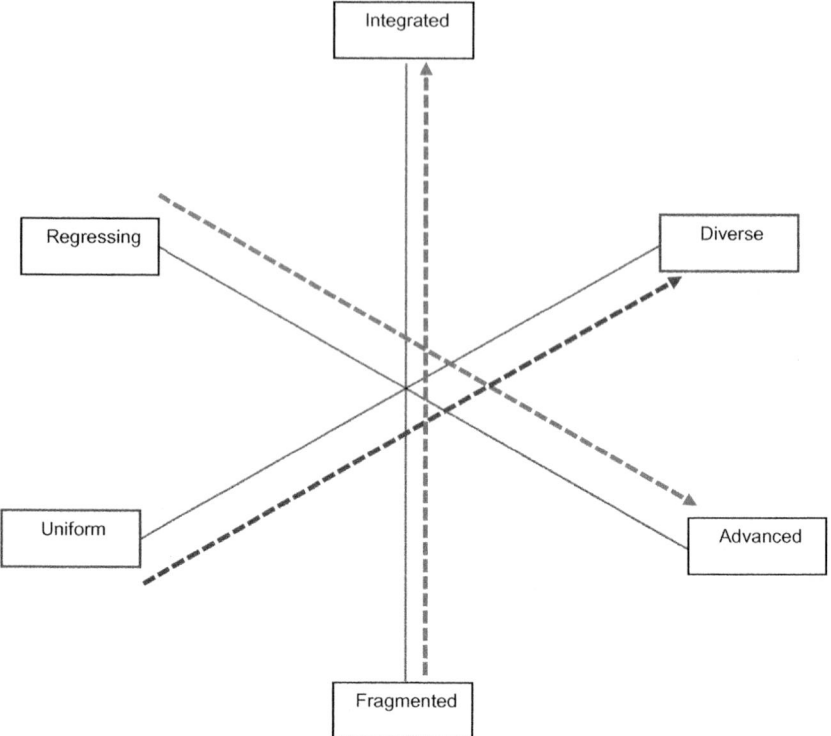

Fig. 1.3 The ideological matrix of China in the 20th and 21st centuries

1.4   ANALYSING CHINESE STATE POLICY

1.4.1   Interpreting Statecraft Through Policy

From within the world-historic paradigm, where states differ from each other is not in the dominant dynamic of unequal exchange with the citizenry, but rather the imperatives for such an arrangement as symbolically constructed in policy. Hence while states are said to be caught up in world capitalism at the moment, their presentation through policy can be expected to vary considerably. By logical extension, parts of the same state may appear more or less similar to others during the same period of time through differences in policy. Furthermore, similarities in symbolic construction could be expected even in policies from different domains such as those under analytical focus in this book: household registration, public service entitlements, language use, and natural disaster management. Overall, the aim of the present study was to make variations in symbolic construction in policy interpretable as *statecraft*, and not how such differences may render policy more or less effective. Also excluded as an aim was the detailed study of commentary on policy in other systems of societal communication such as mass media, except where they were under the control of the state.

Accordingly, the analytical approach to policy was synoptic, whereby instruments of authority across different domains and issued by different organs of the state were jointly read to identify patterns of similarities and differences, the realisations of paradigmatically predicted reproduction. The synoptic approach also involved a comparative element, whereby instruments of authority issued at the central, provincial, municipal, and event sub-municipal levels were read in relation to each other. Thirdly, and by extension, instruments of authority from the same domain and as issued by different municipal or sub-municipal authorities were also read in conjunction. This kind of theoretically informed synoptic approach was also adopted in order to overcome shortcomings identified in the policies studies literature such as the neglect of non-central state actors (Béland, 2019) and inattention to unevenness across localities (Whitworth, 2019).

There were two related analytical foci in the present study within the abovementioned synoptic approach. Attention was paid to variability in ideals of statehood, the citizenry, and nationhood as manifest in policy plus the state imperatives associated with these ideological positions. The present study also concentrated on the reproduction of policy form and of policy function within the same and across domains. The twin foci were helpful to the examination of theoretical contentions derived in the above synthesis of world-historic, action-theoretic, and systems-theoretic insights, and reformulated more concisely, as follows:

1. That state offers to the citizenry vary from policy domain to policy domain, from location to location, group to group, and individual to individual [focus on ideology]
2. That the citizenry is subject to multiple classification schemes in policies across different domains and thereby stratified in no consistently predictable manner [focus on ideology]

3. That the various offers made to the citizenry organised through multiple classification schemes in policy serve to reinforce statehood [focus on ideology]
4. That policy is fragmented as a system of societal communication [focus on policy form and function]
5. That policy is only partially replicated from the past within and between domains [focus on policy form and function]
6. That policy varies in ways which serve to reproduce nationhood.

1.4.2   Focus on Ideology

One use of the ideological matrix introduced in Sect. 1.3.3 is the positioning of policy instruments or parts thereof within it. Differences in ideology between instruments could be illustrated schematically as in Fig. 1.4.

Alternatively, an *ideological shift* within a policy domain could be represented as in Fig. 1.5.

As can be seen in Figs. 1.4 and 1.5, an instrument of authority or policy domain may at the same time contain visions of the state's coherence, progress, and sophistication. Similarly, policy issued by peripheral state organs may contain the above and the equivalents for respective jurisdictions. The ideological matrix can also be employed to identify instances where the central state makes policy explicitly for one part of the territory under its rule. Accordingly, shifts within the matrix may be indicative attempts of easing the tensions between multiple and conflicting imperatives underlying state policies. This assumption was applied not only to contrasting imperatives of the administrative system and those of the economic system underlying positive law (Habermas, 1973/1992), but also to the imperatives within the administrative system itself.

1.4.3   Focus on Policy Form, Function, and Rhetoric

The diversity of measures by which the state reinforces its own existence in a changing geopolitical order implies the need to analyse in detail variations in policy. For such analytical purposes, a series of operational definitions were required for the above contentions to be examined within a synoptic analytical approach, and more fundamentally, on the basis of the present synthesis of world-historic, action-theoretic, and systems-theoretic insights. Apart from ideology, attention was also turned

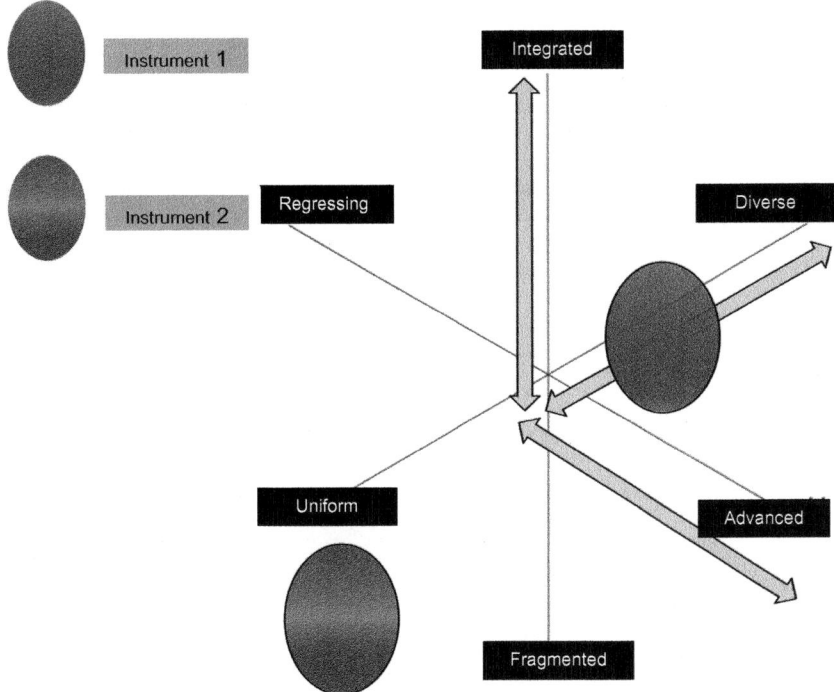

Fig. 1.4 Sample positions of Chinese state policy within the ideological matrix

towards, policy form, policy function, and policy rhetoric. *Form* was defined as the structure of policy and its measures and *function* as the desired outcomes. Over time, policy would leave its legacy ideologically in discursive formations called *rhetoric*. As such, *institutional legacy* may not necessarily be located in explicitly stated contents and objectives, but by discerning more subtly communicated, and partially inherited, ideological positions. Form, function, and rhetoric, while being closely linked, are therefore not required to constitute a uniform contingency in policy-making when the latter comes under analysis.

On the basis of the above working definitions of form, function, and rhetoric, then, the analytical categories of *analogy, hemilogy, heterology,* and *homology* were invoked to characterise the relationship between policy

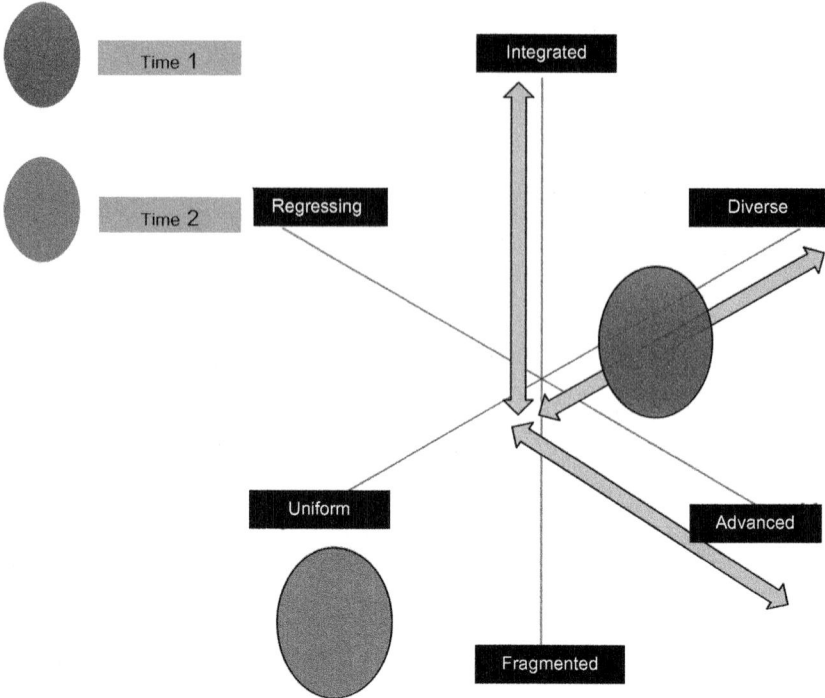

Fig. 1.5 Sample ideological shift among Chinese state policies

instruments, for instance those originating from different levels of administration or from different jurisdictions. Schematically, any two policy instruments from the same policy period could instantiate an analogous, heterologous, hemilogous, or homologous relationship, or none of the above. Analytically, an analogue is the result of partial convergence of policy form and function in spite of the lack of an identical institutional legacy. A homologue, on the other hand, is the consequence of the partial divergence of policy function more so than policy form in spite of a shared institutional legacy. Policies without much of a shared legacy which are also different in form and function are said to be in a heterologous relationship. A hemilogous relationship is somewhat like a homologous one, except the partial divergence is in policy form rather than policy function. These four relationships and corresponding characteristics are summarised

Table 1.1 Comparisons of state policies from the same policy period in terms of legacy, form and function

Relationship between policies	Sharing of institutional legacy	Comparison of policy form	Comparison of policy function
Analogous	Uncommon	Resemblance	Resemblance
Heterologous	Uncommon	Contrast	Contrast
Hemilogous	Common or related	Contrast	Resemblance
Homologous	Common or related	Resemblance	Contrast
Duplicative	*Identical*	*Identical*	*Identical*
Substitutive	Common or related	Contrast	Contrast

in Table 1.1. Note in particular degrees of sharing, convergence, and divergence which distinguish one kind of relationship from another. For comparison, characteristics pertaining to duplication and substitution are shown in addition. Duplication is the intentional and wholesale adoption of earlier policy form, function, and rhetoric. At the other extreme, substitution is the displacement of form, function, and rhetoric which leads to observably new policy.

Over time, the relationship between any two policies is analytically permitted to change, for instance from contrast in structure and/or function to similarity in structure and/or function. Equally, a change from similarity in structure and/or function to contrast in structure and/or function is also analytically conceivable. Both kinds of changes open up the possibility for changes in ideological positions. By extension, these potentially legacy-leaving processes can also be applied to sets of policies during analysis. Permutations stemming from all relationships except duplication and substitution are laid out in a schematic manner in Table 1.2.

The focus on policy form, function, and rhetoric was expected to yield details of the symbolic construction of instruments of authority and of their reproduction across the state. Although such a line of inquiry paralleled the identification of policy layers (cf. Adam et al., 2019) and the tracking of policy direction (cf. Hacker, 2004), there was no intention of conducting the kind of retrospective process-tracing referred to in the policy studies literature (cf. Béland, 2019). Instead, the focus remained on the ideological manner in which nationhood, the citizenry, and statehood are reproduced through policy.

Table 1.2 Changing relationships between state policies

From	To	Comparison of form	Comparison of function
Homology	Homology	Continuity	Continuity
	Hemilogy	Discontinuity	Discontinuity
	Analogy	Continuity	Discontinuity
	Heterology	Discontinuity	Continuity
Hemilogy	Hemilogy	Continuity	Continuity
	Homology	Discontinuity	Discontinuity
	Analogy	Discontinuity	Continuity
	Heterology	Continuity	Discontinuity
Analogy	Analogy	Continuity	Continuity
	Heterology	Discontinuity	Discontinuity
	Homology	Continuity	Discontinuity
	Hemilogy	Discontinuity	Continuity
Heterology	Heterology	Continuity	Continuity
	Analogy	Discontinuity	Discontinuity
	Homology	Discontinuity	Continuity
	Hemilogy	Continuity	Discontinuity

1.5   CHAPTER OUTLINE

In this book, the chapters framed by the introduction and postscript are organised in such a way as to allow a logical presentation of topics and gradual emergence of an analytical account of statecraft as reflected in state policy. The topics cluster around conditions attached by the state to urban residency for internal migrants, and more broadly, membership of the Chinese nation with respect to urban residency. Chapter 2 addresses disparities in household registration requirements resulting from policies made by the municipal governments of Beijing and Suzhou under the central government's campaign to create 100 million new citizens. These disparities are examined against an overview of state policy in the years leading up to 2011, the start of the policy period of concern in the chapter. The overview offers a background against which to consider policies analysed in this and all subsequent chapters. Chapter 3 continues the examination of policy regulation of urban residency by focusing on the provision of publicly funded schooling for children in response to various central government initiatives under the auspices of entitlement equalisation. Unlike the previous chapter, however, this one concentrates on disparities engendered by policy within a single city, namely, the

Municipality of Suzhou. Chapter 4 offers a joint reading of state policies pertaining to urban residency and language use to reveal the state's reasoning for promoting different migration destinations and distances across the nation on account of migrants' command of the *lingua franca* of Putonghua. Chapter 5 deals with publicly funded housing arrangements envisioned by the state in response to two major earthquakes which hit the counties of Wenchuan and Lushan in the Province of Sichuan in 2008 and 2013. As in earlier chapters, the comparative reading of policy documents led to unanticipated disparities not only in respect of urban residency, but rural residency as well. After highlighting the multiple manifestations of statehood, citizenship, and nationhood in China's public policy, the Postscript offers briefly a note on the theoretical and empirical implications of preceding chapters.

Below are summaries of specific analytical problems treated in the empirical chapters of this book. Each analytical chapter will accordingly feature its own elaboration of theoretical, conceptual, and analytical matters raised in introductory sections.

Urban-urban Disparities examined the symbolic architecture of urban residency in China in the period spanning 2011 and 2020. This architecture was interpreted in light of various legacies of state-building dating back to the 1950s, especially the propensity to divide territory and population into symbolic fractions and layering them on top of each other. The symbolic rebuilding of the urban citizenry by means of such fractionalisation was investigated by examining instruments of authority across levels of administration through a focus upon their overlapping forms and functions. While evidently structured by top levels of the state, the campaign to make new urban citizens out of internal migrants was manifest differently in policies made by the Municipality of Beijing and the Municipality of Suzhou. The chapter focused on residential property purchase as an example of policy divergence and identified its inversion from a barrier to an incentive as method of symbolic construction employed by authorities in Suzhou. In this way, different requirements for household registration facing internal migrants were demonstrated across two of China's most popular migration destinations.

Urban Classes examined policy provisions for public service entitlements for the fraction of internal migrant residents in urban areas but without the benefits associated with local household registration. Previously denied access to goods and services such as publicly funded schooling for children, internal migrants became eligible to compete for places in schools in locales they have moved to during the decade ending 2020. As in the reregistration of internal migrants as new citizens, however, such competitions were far from equal. The chapter examined in some depth the official rhetoric of public service entitlement equalisation with local school entry as its main empirical focus. Together with variations in form across districts in Suzhou's urban core, inclusive of Wujiang, recent policy in this domain drew attention to the inequalities instituted by minute symbolic fractions of territory and population, and the choices faced by internal migrants in terms of participation in local economic participation.

Common Tongue and Urban Membership examined policies of the post-1949 Chinese state for signs of nativism, the notion according to which desirable qualities are inalienable from the place of origin. When considered together with the massive urbanisation enterprise definitive of contemporary Chinese society, nativism manifested itself symbolically in ways including policies designed from the 1990s onwards to discourage long-distance internal migration. The promotion of decreased migration distances in policies was also investigated by being read synoptically with policies in the apparently unrelated but intimately connected domain of language use by the Han-speaking majority. What emerged from the analyses in the chapter was however not a clear-cut state position on the native place but an ambivalence to which the citizenry would have to respond to by migrating and even by learning Putonghua.

The final empirical chapter posed the question "Displaced Towards the Urban?" in relation to residents who had to repair or rebuild their places of abode after massive earthquakes in the counties of Wenchuan and Lushan. Despite efforts at the national level in constructing frameworks for natural disaster management, and similarities of the two critical incidents, policy responses to the two earthquakes revealed significant divergence in respect of publicly funded resettlement of residents within both rural and urban areas. The divergence was argued to be due in part to the increased emphasis upon urbanisation as a state project in 2013 when compared to 2008, and the manner in which disaster victims were expected to act differently in order to benefit from state funding. In this way, the chapter demonstrated the effects of policy-making in population management upon that in disaster management.

REFERENCES

Adam, C., Hurka, S., Knill, C., & Steinebach, Y. (2019). *Policy accumulation and the democratic responsiveness trap*. Cambridge University Press.

Béland, D. (2019). *How ideas and institutions shape the politics of public policy*. Cambridge University Press.

Fei, X., Hamilton, G. G., & Wang, Z. (1992). *From the soil: The foundations of Chinese society*. University of California Press.

Fischer, M. (2012). The book of Lord Shang compared with Machiavelli and Hobbes. *Dao-a Journal of Comparative Philosophy, 11*(2), 201–221. https://doi.org/10.1007/s11712-012-9269-y

Habermas, J. (1973/1992). *Legitimation crisis*. Beacon Press.

Habermas, J. (1981a/2005). *The theory of communicative action—One: Reason and the rationalization of society* (T. McCarthy, Trans.). Beacon Press.

Habermas, J. (1981b/2007). *The theory of communicative action—Two: Lifeworld and system* (T. McCarthy, Trans.). Beacon Press.

Habermas, J., & Rehg, W. (1996). *Between facts and norms*. Polity Press.

Hacker, J. S. (2004). Privatizing risk without privatizing the welfare state: The hidden politics of social policy retrenchment in the United States. *American Political Science Review, 98*(2), 243–260. https://doi.org/10.1017/s0003055404001121

Handelman, D. (1995). Cultural taxonomy and bureaucracy in Ancient China: The book of Lord Shang. *International Journal of Politics, Culture, and Society, 9*(2), 263–293. http://www.jstor.org.liverpool.idm.oclc.org/stable/20007238

Harris, R. (Ed.). (2002). *Language myth in western culture*. Routledge.

Hobbes, T. (1651). *Leviathan*. Andrew Crooke.

Hobbes, T., & Tönnies, F. (Eds.). (1889/1928). *The elements of law: Natural and politic*. Cambridge University Press.

Howlett, M., & Rayner, J. (2013). Patching vs packaging in policy formulation: Assessing policy portfolio design. *Politics and Governance, 1*(2), 170–182. https://doi.org/10.17645/pag.v1i2.95

Ingram, H., Schneider, A. L., & deLeon, P. (2007). Social construction and policy design. In P. A. Sabatier (Ed.), *Theories of the policy process* (2nd ed., pp. 93–128). Westview Press.

Kant, I. (1781/1998). *The Cambridge companion to Kant's critique of pure reason* (P. Guyer & A. Wood, Trans.). Cambridge University Press.

Kant, I. (2007). Idea for a universal history with a cosmopolitan aim (1784) (A. W. Wood, Trans.). In G. Zöller & R. B. Louden (Eds.), *Anthropology, history, and education* (pp. 107–120). Cambridge University Press.

Karatani, K. (1993/1998). *Origins of modern Japanese literature* (B. de Bary, Trans.). Duke University Press.

Karatani, K. (2008). Beyond capital-nation-state. *Rethinking Marxism, 20*(4), 569–595. https://doi.org/10.1080/08935690802299447

Karatani, K. (2010/2014). *The structure of world history* (M. K. Bourdaghs, Trans.). Duke University Press.

Karatani, K. (2012/2017). *Isonomia and the origins of philosophy* (J. A. Murphy, Trans.). Duke University Press.

Karatani, K. (2014). *The structure of world history* (M. K. Bourdaghs, Trans.). Duke University Press.

Karatani, K., & Lippit, S. M. (2004/2012). *History and repetition*. Columbia University Press.

Luhmann, N., Kastner, F., & Schiff, D. (Eds.). (1993/2009). *Law as a social system*. Oxford University Press.

Perez, O., & Teubner, G. (Eds.). (2006). *Paradoxes and inconsistencies in the law*. Hart.

Sahlins, M. D. (1976). *Culture and practical reason*. University of Chicago Press.

Sahlins, M. D. (2008). *The western illusion of human nature*. Prickly Paradigm Press.

Shang Yang. (1928). *The book of Lord Shang* (J. J. Duyvendak, Trans.). Probsthain.

Shang Yang. (2017). *The book of Lord Shang* (Y. Pines, Trans.). Columbia University Press.

Teubner, G. (Ed.). (1987). *Autopoietic law: A new approach to law and society*. Walter de Gruyter.

Thelen, K. (2004). *How institutions evolve: The political economy of skills in Germany, Britain, the United States, and Japan*. Cambridge University Press.

Tönnies, F. (1887/2001). *Community and civil society* (J. Harris & M. Hollis, Trans.). Cambridge University Press.

Wallerstein, I. M. (2011a). *The modern world-system* (Vol. IV). University of California Press.

Wallerstein, I. M. (2011b). *The modern world-system* (Vol. III). University of California Press.

Wallerstein, I. M. (2011c). *The modern world-system* (Vol. II). University of California Press.

Wallerstein, I. M. (2011d). *The modern world-system* (Vol. I). University of California Press.

Whitworth, A. (Ed.). (2019). *Towards a spatial social policy*. Policy Press.

CHAPTER 2

Urban–Urban Disparities

Abstract This chapter further develops the paradigmatic perspectives presented in the introductory chapter by sketching out the semiotics of state policy. Emphasis is placed on policy's potential role in facilitating recurring exchanges between the state and society and the means of symbolic construction that such facilitation depends on. Thus elaborated, the same paradigmatic perspectives are employed in the examination of policies by which the Chinese state governs its territory and population. The means of symbolic fractionalisation is shown to be heavily relied upon, not only in the formative years of the People's Republic of China, but more recently in attempts to make internal migrants into new urban citizens. And yet distinctions created by fractionalising territory and population are not always consistently adhered to, and have in fact been added to in new citizenship policies issued by the cities of Beijing and Suzhou. The chapter shows inversion as an additional symbolic means by which the government of Suzhou has exercised an unexpectedly greater degree of selectivity over migrant intake than that of Beijing.

Keywords Citizenship · Differentiation · Political semiotics · State selectivity · Symbolic construction

A wise man creates laws, but a foolish man is controlled by them; a man of talent reforms rites, but a worthless man is enslaved by them. (Shang Yang, 1928, p. 13)

The state is consolidating on a world scale. It weighs down on society (on all societies) in full force; it plans and organizes society 'rationally', with the help of knowledge and technology, imposing analogous, if not homologous, measures irrespective of political ideology, historical background, or the class origins of those in power. (Lefebvre, 1974/1991, p. 19)

The foundation of every division of labour that is well developed, and brought about by the exchange of commodities, is the separation between town and country. (Marx, 1976, p. 506)

2.1   ORIENTATION

Shang Yang, the fourth-century retainer extraordinaire featured in the introductory chapter, would in all likelihood have been regarded as a radical within the context of geopolitical struggles which he sought to shape in favour of his sovereign, Duke Xiao. In an audience granted to him and his supposedly conservative rivals, Shang Yang was at pains to promote reform-based statecraft, drawing on ancient antiquity for precedents of perpetuated rule through variations in rites and laws. In so doing, he trained the focus of such statecraft sharply upon the control of ever greater tracts of territory in northern China through the control of an ever larger share of the population resident there. As Shang Yang was apparently able to convince his patron of the joint outcomes of expansion and stabilisation for the feudal state of Qin, he was later given the authority to introduce wide-ranging reforms in production, consumption, trade, and other aspects of social relations. Given his focus, it was not surprising that his policy agenda, which has survived to this day as *Shang Jun Shu* (1928, 2017), should include varied, interlocking measures applicable to land and people. Somewhat counterintuitively, Shang Yang advocated the diversification of policy not only over time, but within the same period as well. Simply put, he argued for the application of different measures to different parts of the population found in different parts of sovereign territory. In Lefebvre's parlance, Shang Yang had in effect laid out a plan for the production, partly by symbolic means, of space, and beyond that, the production of populace. As each was made symbolically, and remade, neither populace nor space could be homogeneous in any meaningful sense. In turn, this brings into the question any such dichotomous rural–urban formulation as for instance in Karl Marx's (1976, p. 506) unelaborated statement on the origins of commodity exchange through the division of labour. Within the world-historic, action-theoretic, and systems-theoretic paradigms described in the introductory chapter then, the current chapter offers an analysis of governance of territory and population in China in a period of large scale rural-to-urban and urban-to-urban migration. First in this chapter is refinement of the theoretical contentions set out in Sect. 1.4.1. These refinements make more specific the loci, means and processes of symbolic construction, and the derivation of analytical categories associated with them. Next is an overview of intricacies in the rural–urban distinction in state policy up to the year 2011, the start of the policy period in this part of the present study. Included here is a brief excursus on the state's vision of its own policy-making. Attention is then turned analytically to the regulation of migrant populace in the poleis of Beijing and Suzhou, two of the top migrant-attracting municipalities in China, particularly in respect of their permanent settlement in these two urban destinations, and how symbolic construction varied between policy instruments issued by central and respective municipal authorities in service of recent system imperatives despite institutional legacies. Implications for inter-urban disparities in China are presented briefly at the end of the chapter.

2.2   POLICY'S POLITICAL SEMIOTICS

2.2.1   *Reproduction of Exchange Relations Through Recursion*

As already noted in the previous chapter, policy specialists have repeatedly observed the increase in policy density in contemporary society. In studies of policy-making with respect to health care (Hacker, 2004) and social security (Béland, 2007) in the United States, or vocational training there and in Germany and Japan (Thelen, 2004), researchers wrestled with questions of whether policy changes, when it changes, how it changes, and why it changes in spite of the rise in its density. Their debates over the modelling of policy-making notwithstanding, what these researchers could agree to is the rarity of complete displacement of existing policy form, function, and rhetoric. Equally however, in repeatedly being made, policy signals an array of changes in governance, changes which may only seem incremental, but which are nonetheless imperative for the state's continuation. Newer policies or policy measures are added on top of earlier ones in the same domain in what is referred to using the physical metaphor of layering. As it were then, policies are arranged into strata, implying that the institutions they create are also densely compressed together. By taking more of a synoptic, cross-domain approach, researchers such as Adam and colleagues (2019) see a fundamental crisis in governance in ostensibly democratic polities whereby *policy layering* is pervasive enough to result in *policy accumulation*. They argued that nett growth in the number of policy measures, often paradoxically in the name of deregulation, is a sign of policy-making becoming appropriated for electioneering purposes. Further, they reason that layering and accumulation limit rule-by-policy due to the sheer impossibility of implementing incommensurate measures through impenetrable institutions. Ironically, in such an environment, indistinct political promises proliferate more so than genuinely novel policy measures actually carrying the potential to deliver outcomes.

Paradigmatically, there are several reasons to hypothesise the same political semiotics for China's public policy despite differences in polity. If for no other reason than its participation in world capitalism, the Chinese state can be expected to also have its government reconfigure symbolically relations of similarity and difference through policy-making. Where China stands out from other states may not be in the practice of layering as such, to take an example of a policy process, but rather the precise manner in which policies are layered, and the political functions served by layering. Irrespective of the actual manner of the purpose of layering, policy-as-symbolic-construction is in effect *recursive* (cf. Karatani & Lippit, 2004/2012).

Secondly, policification, the non-legislative counterpart of juridification, is expected of the Chinese state in the period of concern, namely from 2011 to 2020. Policification is not merely the increase in the amount of regulation potentially involving layering and accumulation, but also the further penetration of system into lifeworld. How far lifeworld has become absorbed into system remains a question, one that has received little attention in these theoretical terms with contemporary China as the empirical focus. What seems helpful as a hypothetical starting point is the observation of bureaucratic desiccation in a public sphere featuring both juridification and policification (cf. Habermas, 1981/2007, p. 386).

Such policy-based divisions structure symbolically not only political deliberations, but also the populace which the deliberations are presumably concerned with. As shall be evident later in this chapter, even poleis are subject to such intricate cross-classification in public policy regulating internal migration. Bureaucratic desiccation of territory, population, and resettlement is made possible, it would appear, by increasingly delicate permutations of policy form, function, and rhetoric.[1] As such, policy-as-symbolic-construction, apart from being recursive, is also reductive and selective.

Thirdly, as policy-as-symbolic-construction is evidently reproductive while also being reductive and selective, it gives rise to lineages over time. The biological metaphor of reproduction, which remains nothing more than a metaphor, can be extended to underscore both similarity and differences as policy recurs selectively, and reduces its objects selectively. For these purposes, four analytical categories of analogy, hemilogy, heterology, and homology,[2] which stem from the hypothetical variations in form, function, and rhetoric (see Sect. 1.4.3), are meant to provide broader coverage of possibilities in symbolic recursion in policy-making than what is possible with those already in the policy studies literature, namely first-order, second-order, and third-order policy changes (Hall, 1993), policy conversion, policy layering (e.g. Béland, 2007; Thelen, 2004), and policy drift (e.g. Hacker, 2004). With recursion analytically elaborated with the four categories, the policies in question can be positioned within the ideological matrix along the dimensions of coherence, progress, and sophistication (see Sect. 1.4.2). In so doing, symbolic recursion in policy-making can be further interpreted as recursion of modes of exchange, and the political order these modes support. What becomes theoretically possible at this point are the prospects of different dominant modes of exchange across localities, and different dominant modes of exchange between segments of the population, all within the same nation.

---

[1] As they are employed in the present study, the rubrics of form, function and rhetoric, subsume the ones in policy studies, such as Peter Hall (1993)'s set of three. Respectively, the above correspond approximately to policy instrument form and measures, policy goals, and policy setting.

[2] The analytical categories of *analogy, hemilogy, heterology* and *homology* were derived from pre-Darwin studies of animal anatomy and exemplified by the work of Robert Owen (Owen & White Cooper, 1843). Commitment to evolutionary biology is neither the premise here nor is there any need for such commitment in advancing the study of policy as a kind of societal communication.

Hence apart from rewriting itself upon itself, policy is meant to rewrite as its other locus exchange relations recursively as it seeks to govern the state's population and territory, and in the process, reproduce its objects.

2.2.2   Differentiation by Fractionalisation

The mostly selective and usually reductive reproduction of policy objects in symbolic recursion can be identified within different units of analysis. Reproduction can be seen in state policy in an over-arching, and abstract sense, or more tangibly, within a policy domain demarcated using criteria provided by the state or by the analyst, each with its own empirical implications. Even more tangibly, analysis refers to discrete instruments of authority issued publicly by different levels of government, and within the polity being examined in the present study, instruments made public by the Communist Party of China. An individual policy document, it has to be stressed, is itself a relative unit of communication. No straightforward explanation is necessarily available for its length, its media content if any, or its means of circulation if multiple. Hence while the document presented as having its own provenance is a unit of analysis, it would not be the only unit of analysis. Within the document it might be tantalising to engage in parsing, but against the advice given by the unwitting founder of discourse analysis: "one determines neither a lexical organization, nor the scansions of a semantic field" (Foucault, 1971/1972). For lexical organisation, or some other level of language description only captures part of policy form, and in turn, policy form is only one part of how policy varies. The paradigmatic reasoning informing the present study's conduct requires flexibility in the unit of analysis so that ideological abstractions, semiotic minutiae, and everything in between, can all be admissible. This is especially so given the hypothesised tendency of state policy to differentiate within its own terms rather than to delete or transform them entirely. For greater clarity, symbolic differentiation increasing in delicacy internally will henceforth be referred as *fractionalisation*, while that which increases in delicacy externally will be labelled as *opposition*. Dividing inward or multiplying outward respectively, both of these means of symbolic construction result in either overlapping *sets* or contrasting *types*. Fractionalisation might, but does not always result in objects organised explicitly as a hierarchy. Although opposition makes exclusion ever more salient, unlike fractionalisation, it does not thereby create new objects as such. Entirely new objects independent of the terms of existing policy are conceivable, such as objects adopted into policy from other sub-systems of societal communication (cf. Luhmann et al., 1993/2009). Figure 2.1 illustrates these means of symbolic construction with elaborations on differentiation in particular.

Fractionalisation and opposition, like most other means of symbolic construction, are assumed to continue beyond the first iteration. They recur, that is to say, continue to repeat themselves partially, showing not only similarities but differences in addition. Hence objects arising from fractionalisation might subsequently be subject to further change by means of opposition, and vice versa. The incomplete and serial aspects of policy change have to date not been conceptualised at this level of detail in policy studies, possibly due to the preponderance of relatively larger units of analysis above the document level (see Adam et al., 2019). Elsewhere, in anthropological linguistics, Susan Gal and Judith Irvine (2019) offered the conceptual device of *fractal recursion*, with which they accounted for the incomplete reproduction of ideological biases across

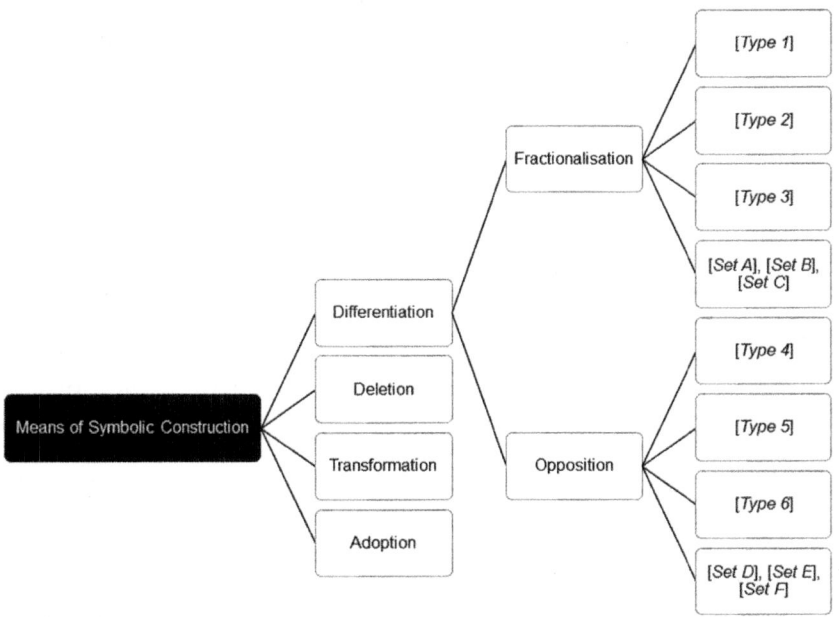

Fig. 2.1 Major means of symbolic construction in Chinese state policy

disparate contexts. For the current chapter, it is especially significant that their illustrations should revolve around the recursion of social evaluations based originally on a distinction between artisans and farmers in a country town in Hungary. This distinction, and evaluations based on them, was argued by these authors to be appropriated in other contexts, including urban ones during Hungary's post-communist era (Gal, 2016). The farmer–artisan distinction in the country town eventually became a distinction between communism and liberalism in the capital, a fractal correspondence that was not actual as such, but perceptible in a different time and place. In other words, a socio-economic rural-rural distinction was recontextualised into a political rural–urban distinction, and on a larger scale. The same ideological preferences in respect of livelihood as those from the town were to find new expression in previously unmade comparisons outside the original context. The many instances of recursion in social life that Gal and Irvine conceptualised with a single term are supposedly fractal in the sense that when in comparison with each other, they increase or decrease in scale, in addition to being imperfect images of each other.

As mathematician Bonoit Mandelbrot (1983) indicated, fractals were conceptualised initially in order to allow chaotic irregularities to be described in terms of scalable relations, and potentially, explained. In Mandelbrot's account, fractals had been so applied not only to irregular shapes found in nature, but also noises, movements as well as human abstractions such as word frequencies and market prices. Despite the wide range of applications in the natural and social world, Mandelbrot cautioned against fractal description as a pretext for positivist laws of either world (Mandelbrot et al., 2013). Nonetheless, these conceptual attempts to grapple with the ongoing but shifting duplication of fragments parallel the present ones to investigate the transposition of ideologically charged fractions in policy-making between the domains of household registration, public service entitlements, language use, and natural disaster management. As fractals do not in themselves refer to a single class of scaling phenomena, reference will continue to be made to recursion, rather than fractal recursion as Gal and Irvine did. What Gal and Irvine have added to the mathematical study of fractals is the highlighting of human agency in symbolic reproduction, a consideration that will be manifest not only in the following overview of how the Chinese state differentiated land, people and residency in policy, but also in further analytical categories in later chapters of this book.

Recurring fractionalisation and opposition across policy documents establish relations between symbols that are scalable in the sense of involving authorities at different levels of government, authorities with different remits at the same level, authorities at the same level with different jurisdictions, and instruments of authority layered on earlier ones with a different scope. These variations between policy documents occur along a geographical scale and simultaneously, a temporal scale. Accordingly, for instance, elements of centrally issued policy can be expected to be found in locally issued policy, and vice versa, while apparent policy innovations can be shown to be incomplete iterations of past measures (cf. Campbell, 2002). Researchers have attempted to capture such complexity in policy processes by making use of the extended metaphors of "palimpsest" (e.g. Carter, 2012) and "policyscape" (e.g. Mettler, 2016). Respectively, these picture policy as the very medium for reinscribing rule upon itself repeatedly, and as previous changes to the political environment which now act to constrain further developments. Conceptually, uses of these metaphors tend to highlight the unevenness which results from symbolic recursion, irrespective of the actual loci, means and processes of such recursion. As a way of taking stock of the above metaphors given the paradigmatic concerns of the present volume, under examination in the next section are those elements of Chinese state policy which were to remain in different ways as textual and political sediments (cf. Luhmann et al., 1993/2009) which sustain urban-urban disparities during the years spanning 2011 and 2020.

2.3   Poleis and Populace in China

2.3.1   Mutual Imbrication of Territory and Population in Policy

Segmentation of land and the people who live upon it is not peculiar to any particular period of any one nation's history. By means and processes of symbolic construction in Chinese antiquity land tenure systems were invented only to be reinvented. Partly as a result, people within the national fold were classified repeatedly. For instance, in the Warring States period Shang Yang (1928, 2017) advocated to the ruler of the Qin state policy proposals that were aimed at raising the productivity of peasants, securing food for forces on foreign expeditions while also limiting the affluence of aristocrats. Qin was at the time outperformed by neighbouring states in terms of both its arable land and farming population.

Among other things, Shang Yang's policy proposals entailed incentives to migrate across state borders into Qin that were predicated on time-bound exemption from military service and taxes and promises of land tenure. Hence insofar as inbound migration was concerned, the population was fractionalised in terms of the length of affiliation with the state and simultaneously of occupation in the same state.[3] Subjects would accordingly concentrate on warfare while migrants would focus on agriculture for at least four generations. Beyond this point in the process, former migrants and their descendants were committed by policy to agriculture unless their participation in warfare was required. Notably, Shang Yang advised against internal migration in order that even waste lands would be productively cultivated.[4] Far from a stable taxonomy with rigid categories, Shang Yang was trying to institute politically purposive reclassification of the population in addition to its cross-classification. Rather than forming contrasting types therefore, Shang Yang's categories of "farmer" and "soldier" overlapped at any given point in time and also over time. He also proposed further fractionalisation of the "soldier" category into three types, one consisting of able-bodied men, another of able-bodied women, and lastly one of adults fitting other descriptions.[5]

Territory, like population, was subject to fractionalisation into sets of overlapping elements. Shang Yang sought to redraw jurisdictional boundaries within the state of Qin by combining small cities, towns and villages into *xian* (county, 县), a unit of administration whose form and function was to change over the course of history. Into *xian* even enfeoffments were absorbed according to policies promoted by Shang Yang.[6] As with occupation, jurisdiction was fractionalised recursively rather than rigidly. However, despite changes in scale relative to other units of administration, in *xian* an enduring model was established of local governance by the central state that is still evident in China today (L. Li, 2020; Shang Yang, 1928, see commentary by Jan Duyvendak on p. 18). Like *jun* (commandery or prefecture, 郡), *xian* was conceived of in antiquity

---

[3] See especially the chapter entitled *Encouragement of Immigration*.

[4] See especially the chapter entitled *Order to Cultivate Waste Lands*.

[5] See especially the chapter entitled *Military Defence*.

[6] See *Basic Annals of the State of Qin* and *The Biography of Shang Jun* in *Shiji*, available at https://ctext.org/shiji. Burton Watson's translation, which appeared as *Records of the Grand Historian of China*, did not contain these chapters.

as an administrative division whose population included not only artisans and farmers, but soldiers as well.[7] As such, neither rural nor urban
districts formed the centre of administration; the two kinds of district
were distinguished politically by land use and the occupations taken up
by the population. The county, as least in antiquity, was meant territori-
ally to be an integrated unit administered by officials acting on behalf of
the central state. In having elements of the rural and the urban embedded
within it by policy, the Chinese county stood in contrast from the ancient
Greek poleis.[8]

Territorial fractions in China had been observed not only in the form
of horizontal divisions, but also vertical ones as well. Particularly pertinent was Fei Xiaotong's (1939) analysis of what had remained of absentee
landlordship in eastern and southern China during the republican period
(1911–1949). According to Fei, this kind of absentee landlordship in
locations such as Suzhou was possible on the basis of fractionalisation
of arable land into the surface and the notional subsoil beneath it. Tenure
was thus differentiated into entitlements to the surface on the one hand,
and entitlements to the subsoil on the other. The surface was leased or
tenanted, usually for the purpose of cultivation, and never sold, while
purchases could have been made and were made for the subsoil. Taxes
were levied on holders of subsoil titles in principle, but paid in practice by
tenants, who differed from lessees in having permanent rights to cultivate
the surface. Fei reasoned that arable land in the two river delta regions was
sufficiently productive to attract capital inflows from towns into nearby
villages. When combined with highly complex allotment practices then,
the tenure categories of landlords, tenants, and lessees were not "clear-cut
or water-tight classes" (Fei, 1939, p. 192). In the tumult of the period
(see Sect. 4.2.2), tensions were building between towns and villages not
only in these river delta regions, but in the rural heartlands of interior
provinces also. As Fei astutely observed, tenure reform proposals from
this period were mostly based on state realignment of land ownership by
the populace with cultivation, or effectively the symbolic erasure of any
distinction between the surface and the subsoil. If Shang Yang's tenure-
granting measure were to be considered as a political sediment, republican

---

[7] Duyvendak (Shang Yang, 1928) rendered jun (郡) into prefecture and *xian* (县),
sub-prefecture in the chapter entitled *Fixing of Rights and Duties*.

[8] That is, πόλις.

period tenure reform proposals would appear as attempts to bring the state into a more prominent role in exchange relations involving the rural and peri-rural population.

2.3.2 Symbolic Construction of Poleis in Policy

Territorial fractions in post-1949 China also reflected the same historical concern with entrenching the central state in local rule. These fractions were written in different ways into the Constitution of the People's Republic of China, which itself went through multiple iterations since being first enacted in 1954.[9] The Constitution created rural and urban fractions of territory, and within urban fractions, those of different sizes. Other than the national capital of Beijing, no other jurisdiction is named in the Constitution. All other instruments of authority, which in principle stem from the Constitution, offer additional means of fractionalising jurisdictions. Such means of symbolic construction have important implications upon what constitutes the urban in state policy, and the corresponding justifications for differential policy treatments of the population resident in territorial fractions deemed to be urban in different ways.

Whereas the 1954 constitution stipulated that "Cities directly under central government jurisdiction and other large cities consist of districts", since the 1978 Constitution these cities were fractionalised not only into districts, but into "districts and counties". While districts were clearly urban in the sense of being constituent fractions of a city, the urban status of counties was far more ambiguous, especially considering counties in the 1950s as sites of both farmland redistribution and economic collectivisation (King, 1977), and three decades later, as those of agricultural de-collectivisation (Ho, 2006). Although some researchers have identified 1978 as a point at which the relationship between counties and cities was reconfigured and institutionalised by the central state (e.g. Cartier & Hu, 2020), provisions beyond the Constitution for the rescaling of central state interventions through local jurisdictions had already been made two decades earlier (National People's Congress, 1959). To be sure, the 1959 provisions, which allowed the leadership of counties by cities, were

---

[9] Four constitutions were enacted by National People's Congress, respectively in 1954, 1975, 1978, and 1982. Amendments to the 1982 constitutional document were approved by the same organ in 1988, 1993, 1999, 2004 and 2018.

broadly worded, in effect to have facilitated the accommodation of vast differences in political economy across space and time. The key quali-fication of size in the 1959 reference to "large cities" had never been explicitly defined. Literally expressed as "relatively larger cities",[10] this constitutional formulation was to prove crucial in the symbolic construc-tion of multiple scales along which jurisdictions were ranked into tiers under different circumstances. Hence since the late 1970s and early 1980s counties could both be on par with cities as per the constitution and yet, subordinate to cities as per other post-1954 instruments of authority. The constitutional parity between counties and cities was not thereby negated, however, as it subtly served as the basis of provincial authorities exer-cising leadership over counties, even those formally under cities deemed sufficiently large for particular policy objectives (cf. T. Zhou, 2014). The subordination of counties to a prefecture-level city and to its superordi-nate provincial authority had been observed for example with respect to Suzhou (Cartier & Hu, 2020), whose status as a "larger" city was not ratified formally until 1993 (State Council, 1993), and whose inbound migration policies is the empirical focus of this chapter.

The symbolic construction of Suzhou as a larger city incorporating surrounding counties highlights the role of the state in "separation between town and country" (Marx, 1976, p. 506). At least since the 1950s, the Chinese state had been crafting differentiations between the rural and the urban to achieve a variety of governance objectives. Specifications of land ownership in the Constitution (National People's Congress, 1982), which for the first time delineated "land in cities" from "land in rural and suburban areas", were soon to pave the way for the state to reclassify the latter into the former (e.g. State Council, 1985, 1986), with profound implications for the political economy of the jurisdictions concerned, the nation, and the world. Both in legal policy (National People's Congress, 2019a, 2019b) and administrative policy (State Council, 2021), the mid-1980s saw the return of the fractionali-sation of tenure into usage of the surface and ownership of sub-surface. Unlike absentee landlordship in rural China during the republican period (Fei, 1939; King, 1977), however, land in cities is public in the sense of state ownership of the sub-surface, which the Constitution equates with

---

[10] That is, 较大的市 (jiàodàdeshì).

ownership "by the people" (National People's Congress, 2018). Furthermore, non-state usage of urban land surface, including the purchase and sale thereof, is limited to zones to which state planning has already been applied. Hence policy fractionalises land in cities further into elements for which state planning exists, and for which the state proscribes non-state uses. Article 2 of *Regulation on the Implementation of the Land Administration Law*, first enacted in 1998, states:

> Land development, protection, and construction activities shall insist on the principle of planning coming first. Territorial spatial plans approved in accordance with the law shall be the primary basis for various activities of development, protection, and construction. (State Council, 2021)

As has been noted by researchers, such latitude for state action in land use through urban planning is intentionally institutionalised in policy overall (Ho, 2006) and in localities such as Suzhou (Pieke, 2009).

It was hardly a coincidence that the dictum "reform and opening up" made its way to the preamble to the Constitution in amendments passed in 1993 (National People's Congress, 1993), amendments which also saw references to "planned economy" replaced by "socialist market economy". Provisions for varying rural–urban dynamics from the late 1970s onwards were made when the state placed the Chinese nation on a vehicle towards development that was meant to be fuelled by urbanisation. As illustrated by the gradual reorganisation of eight counties into four county-level cities under Suzhou between 1989 and 1995 (Cartier & Hu, 2020), urbanisation in this short period of reform was very much policy-induced, and featured not only changes expected to the state-society dynamic, and the rural–urban dynamic, but also the dynamics between local authorities seeking to or asked to operate at a different level by central authorities (Ma, 2005). The cities-within-a-city formation thus established was replicated elsewhere in China, creating a cascade of patterns akin to multiple Russian-doll fractal[11] recursions (Rosenfeld & Nordahl, 2016). There were several major statistical effects of this kind of urbanisation-by-policy in China: the relatively rapid increase in the proportion of land in cities, and along with that, enlargement of planned urban areas; the proportion of the population resident in cities; and not insignificantly, the proportion of urban residents with demand for

---

[11] That is, a Matrëshka fractal.

housing. While these figures represented aggregate growth nation-wide, the growth was not evenly distributed across all urban territorial fractions created by policy.

2.3.3 Symbolic Construction of Populace in Policy

The intricate symbolic construction of poleis in China since the 1980s is crucial in examining the equally delicate symbolic construction of populace in the same period. Not only does the imbrication of territory and population in policy imply cross-classification of both, it also indicates the symbolic construction of one in terms of the other. Policy classification resulted in the placement of population within nested, quasi-territorial categories, namely those of the rural populace and urban populace. Conversely, the constitutional ranking of cities by size since 1978 had effectively allowed the resident population to serve as one of many criteria by which to define urban scale. Cities with larger populations were more highly placed and still tend to be more highly placed in different systems of ranking.

In the same way that policy had repeatedly renewed the definition of land in cities, it did the same with people in cities. Symbolically, people in cities could be so on account of their residency in an urban jurisdiction, as for instance in a county levelled upward to a county-level city. Increasingly since the 1980s, however, people were deemed to be in cities on account of their occupation, and specifically non-involvement in agriculture. Direction of policy was then shifting gradually to a combination of controlling and promoting the movement of rural migrants into urban areas for the purposes other than agriculture (Huang, 2013; Young, 2013). The vast majority of these migrants were holders of agricultural household registration records, meaning that they had had their *de jure* places of residence set in localities which were at the time rural jurisdictions. *De facto* residence on land in cities presented a number of symbolic challenges to governance when contrasted with *de jure* residence in the same location by other members of the populace. First and foremost, nationhood, which the Constitution exemplifies, implies political kinship of the entire domestic population. Secondly, land in cities is owned implicitly by "by the people" via the state itself (National People's Congress, 2018) irrespective of geographical origins. Thirdly, unlike territory, the Constitution makes no provision for the administrative division of population based on the type of economic output, whether presumed or actual.

Lastly, expansion of non-primary industries during reform and opening up required a much greater inbound labour force than what urban jurisdictions already catered to, and were able to support, in terms of public goods and services. Without full-time agricultural occupation as a differentiator, in what ways could statehood be manifest in policy in terms of maintaining political kinship for all, actualising rights to the city, ensuring labour supply and fulfilling public service obligations during the course of accelerated urbanisation?

The mere designation of migrant-residents in contradistinction from more established residents in cities is sufficiently indicative of the difficulties in symbolic differentiation of the populace in the years leading up to 2011. In policy documents, differentiation occurs in part by adding qualifications to the term *min*,[12] which by itself connotes people in general and subjects of the state in particular. However, none of the constructions *renmin* (human-people),[13] *guomin* (nation-people),[14] or *gongmin* (public-people)[15] would fully serve the purpose of signalling any particular fraction of the urban population. The term *renmin* had since 1949 been associated with the identity of the state and its institutions, being found for instance in the designation "People's Republic of China". With the term *guomin*, state policy habitually refers to matters of importance that involve the populace in its entirety, as for instance in the expression *guomin jingji* (nation-people economy),[16] in the title *Five-year Plan of the Economy and Society*, a key statement of state policy issued periodically since 1953. Of the three terms, only *gongmin* is used to describe people in *Regulation of Household Registration* (National People's Congress, 1958), one of the key documents underlying the policy of controlled labour migration into cities. Most commonly rendered in English as "citizen", a symbol of equity in rights, *gongmin* tended to be replaced by the demographically loaded term of *renkou*[17] (population) in subsequent policies in the same domain. Population was fractionalised into that which

---

[12] That is, 民 (mín).

[13] That is, 人民 (rénmín).

[14] That is, 国民 (guómín).

[15] That is, 公民 (gōngmín).

[16] That is, 国民 (guómín jīngjì).

[17] That is, 人口 (rénkǒu).

presumably engaged in agriculture[18] and that which presumably did not engage in agriculture,[19] both presumptions being made on the basis of the *de jure* place of residence (e.g. State Council, 1981). The same qualifications were extended in the 1990s to make up household registration attributes, again with the line being drawn along presumed involvement or non-involvement in agriculture.[20] This differentiation was not at all sustainable given the non-agricultural activities of rural migrants headed for cities. As a way out of the symbolic quagmire, people living in some cities were subsumed under the category of *jumin* (residents)[21] irrespective of jurisdictional origins or their links to agriculture (e.g. Municipality of Suzhou, 2007). In everyday discourse, which had already been shaped by decades of household registration policy, *jumin* once meant the fraction of urban residents distinguishable from *nongmin* (peasants).[22] Hence the inclusion of agricultural household registrants into the urban fold in some urban jurisdictions was notable as the symbolic removal of the socioeconomic identity associated with rural origins. Nonetheless, as shown by later developments in policy, the designation of internal migrants as urban residents did not in itself resolve completely the tensions between objectives underlying state-sponsored urbanisation. The potency of differentiation in ordering land-use and labour notwithstanding, additional means of symbolic construction were needed to prevent policy from excessive layering and eventual dysfunction.

2.4 Discursive Architecture as Statecraft

2.4.1 *The State as a Visionary*

Discretionary and incremental changes are not the only kind of action the state engages in through policy as has been suggested by researchers of Chinese state policy (Ho, 2006; Young, 2013). The Chinese adage

---

[18] That is, 农业人口 (nóngyè rénkǒu).

[19] That is, 非农业人口 (fēinóngyè rénkǒu).

[20] Respectively, 农业户口性质 (nóngyè hùkǒu xìngzhì) and 非农业户口性质 (fēinóngyè hùkǒu xìngzhì).

[21] That is, 居民 (jūmín).

[22] That is, 农民 (nóngmín).

of "crossing the river by feeling for stones"[23] has often been used to read pragmatism into such policy. As paradigmatically policy exists in order for the state to structure exchange relations, it is theoretically more germane that the state should present itself as having any long-term vision at all. This seems to be so because any vision could potentially commit the state to actions it cannot take or no longer wishes to take under unforeseen circumstances in the future. Even as the legislature and government were inducing internal migration in the urban direction by means of various prefecture-level policy experiments at the turn of the millennium (Chan & Buckingham, 2008; Wallace, 2014), the Communist Party of China was concurrently reinforcing the ideological bases for the even broader undertaking of reform and opening up. Several dicta were invented by the Party during under the leadership of Hu Jintao for these purposes, of which *The Scientific Outlook on Development*[24] was eventually elaborated from a concept into a treatise on China's future (Central Committee of the Communist Party of China, 2013). The treatise takes as its own basis a view of development as being founded on immutable, objective, and scientific principles. According to these principles, improvement in the following three respects would act as China's panacea: the unleashing of productivity, enhancing of national capacity, and fulfilling of ever-increasing needs of the masses. Particular mention was made of the masses' "material and cultural" needs, a reference to the consumptive aspirations of the populace. Stemming from these principles is the notion of "human-centredness",[25] which when applied to policy would make equality in participation by the masses in China's modernisation a new priority. Implicitly then, comprehensive improvement would mean the lifting of both production and consumption by the masses. With additional symbolic constructions from the treatise then, the state acknowledged rather explicitly the major dilemma of social inequality and the path to extrication from this dilemma. The state's role in effecting

---

[23] That is, 摸着石头过河 (mōzhē shítóu guòhé), an expression which official media noted was used by but not invented by former state leader Deng Xiaoping. See for example http://cpc.people.com.cn/n1/2018/0412/c69113-29921565.html.

[24] That is, 科学发展观 (kēxué fāzhǎn guān). As a notion, this was introduced at the 16th Party Congress in 2002, written into the Constitution of the CPC in the 17th Party Congress in 2007 and in the 18th Party Congress in 2012.

[25] That is, 以人为本 (yírén wéibén), often rendered in unofficial translations as "putting people first".

continuous growth is portrayed in *The Outlook* as being just as funda-mental as the masses' needs. In keeping both human need and historical end in view, the Party had effectively articulated its understanding of perpetual state-society exchange as a condition of both polity and policy. In other words, the entire nation's existence is predicated upon state guar-antee of the well-being of the entire population within its territory. Under the ideological influence of Party policy then, legislative and administra-tive policy decreasingly cast internal migration as disorder and increasingly as potential. Whereas internal migrants from a rural background were presented as excess productive capacity in policy in the 1980s, by the 2000s they were symbolically made a core, albeit distinct, constituency of labour supply in the nation. By the new millennium, the designation "peasant-migrant worker" (*nongmingong*)[26] had made its way into policy discourse. It would not be until the policy period in question, that is the years spanning 2011 and 2020, when rural origins, and the disadvantage they imply in urban residency, were more decisively dealt with by symbolic means.

Paradigmatically, party pronouncements, legislative enactments, and government regulations up to the year 2011 had made ever more evident the commodification of both land and labour under world capitalism. Delicate fractions had been derived from both, and in turn these frac-tions were intricately linked to each other through policy measures. These criss-crossing, inter-dependent differentials are crucial to the creation of surplus value through the steering medium of money. Theoretically, the official vision for China set out is one of capital accumulation through the mobility of its citizens, not only in rural-to-urban labour migration, but also for many, in the maintenance of dual residency and economic specialisation within individual households. As part of reform and opening up, the rural–urban divide instituted through land tenure stipulations in the Constitution no longer translates into a problem of stemming the tide of population along a single socio-economic gradient, and becomes instead one of exploiting the sheer force of this tide for the generation of capital. The Party's logic by which land, people, stability, and wealth are connected is not difficult to discern. As with land reforms in the

---

[26] That is, 农民工 (nóngmíngōng), literally "peasant-worker". The "peasant-migrant worker" adds the attribute of relocation as a way putting the demographic into its histor-ical context. Like any demographic, however, its socioeconomic diversity cannot possibly be accommodated by any given expression.

1950s, economic reforms since the 1980s were a matter of imbuing geography with culturally accepted but uneven value, representing the latter as prices while promoting investment *en masse* as the resultant market would allow. In the early 1950s wealth for the rural population was in the form of above-subsistence living from labour invested on small plots distributed by the state. By the 2000s, wealth was manifest in the purchase of residential property built on land in cities with funds derived from non-agricultural labour or other sources. The two periods of reform differ not in the kinds of resources mobilised by the state for nation-building, but rather in the means by which geographical capital and human capital are converted into monetary capital, and vice versa, as well as in the interventions by the state in capital conversion processes. Shang Yang's shrewd observation in antiquity remains relevant today to exchanges between the state and the citizenry (Shang Yang, 1928, p. 222):

> *a sage's way of ordering a country, is that the people's capital should be stored in the soil and that dangers would be run abroad by borrowing a temporary habitat.*

That capital could be generated from variable permutations of land and people is a principle of political economy reflected in policy even before reform and opening up. As the Party itself would claim, its policy is the crystallisation of collective wisdom, or less euphemistically, the filtering of past experiences in managing state–society relations, a kind of state-led policy layering. Large-city status, which as mentioned earlier in this chapter was enshrined in the 1954 Constitution, became operationalised in 1978 in terms of population figures by the forerunner of the Ministry of Housing and Urban–Rural Development[27] (Huang, 2013; Sahlins, 1976). The 1978 division between large, medium, and small cities was based on the size of the ordinarily resident population. Penchant for demographic magnitude and the opportunity for betterment connected to it was presumed by policy-designers of migrants.[28] Hence a pattern was set even then in internal migration policy whereby the strictest controls were to be exercised in the most populous urban

---

[27] Then known as the National Construction Commission.

[28] Ma (2005) had previously observed the same penchant among officials in rural jurisdictions although it was unclear what the observation was based on.

jurisdictions. By the same logic, the smallest of cities, in being presumably least attractive and least expensive, did not require as many controls and not to the same degree. In turn, less stringent measures were meant to prevent concentration of migrants in large urban centres in numbers beyond their capacity. Just like the ambiguity over urban scale in the 1954 Constitution, urban capacity for residents remains unspecified in official policy documents published since 1979. Researchers affiliated with the State Council alluded nonetheless to the use of urban land area figures and population density figures as the basis for construing urban capacity (e.g. in the prefecture-level city of Changsha, see Jin, 2015). In any case, preoccupation with urban magnitude by whatever measure is commensurate with the teleology of development later spelt out by the Party in *The Outlook*. Equally significant as the Party's long-term aspirations for China is its envisioning of uneven development across urban spaces and among urban residents. The above suggests a statecraft informed by the system imperative of national growth through uneven local development, an imperative discernible in policy when it is placed under analysis.

2.4.2 The State as Top-Level Designer

Nonetheless, in the ideological spirit of *The Outlook*, uneven development of China is the incomplete development of China. Leadership of the Party and the state would accordingly have to carry development to its ideological conclusion of equality. In the more abstract realm of visions at least, inequality is a complex problem to be solved rather than a practical compromise to be accepted and forgotten. Faced with such a seemingly intractable problem, Party leaders attempted to further explain their vision by means of extended metaphors. These metaphors have in common references to comprehensive mastery and adaptive strategy in state affairs. One key metaphor popularised since the 10th Five-year Plan period (2001–2005)[29] in policy circles was that of "top-level design", an official interpretation of which was offered on the occasion of the approval of the 12th Five-year Plan in March 2011 (The Editors of Xinhuanet, 2011) and also in the 12th Five-year Plan itself (National People's Congress, 2011). The imagery is one of establishment and reworking of systems within which institutions of the state, inclusive of

---

[29] That is, 顶层设计 (dǐngcéng shèjì).

the Party, the legislature and government, carry out their daily operations. As such, top-level design is not concerned with tangible targets for the short term, already the subject of documents such as five-year plans. Nor is top-level design a matter of directly altering institutions, each of which is already the legacy of decades of policy-making. Rather, top-level design is meant to bridge gaps between major state institutions that are inevitable in invariably varied policy and its implementation. In so doing, the overall vision of betterment for all is more likely to be realised in spite of inter-locking constraints set up through policy and competing demands of policy actors. As co-ordinator then, top-level leaders design and redesign the nation-state into a coherence which neither vision nor operation alone would bring about. Accordingly, conditions for equality would have to be progressively constructed, even if a lengthy and uncertain process.

2.4.3   A New Identity for an Old Dilemma

Although by the new millennium the term "peasant-migrant workers" had lost much of its epithetic properties in everyday use, its entry into policy documents concerning or with implications on household registration was not resonant with the rhetoric being promoted by the Party at the time. Similarly, alternatives like "transient population"[30] and "non-native labouring personnel"[31] were on the verge of becoming anachronistic. At the very least, a new identity was needed to acknowledge demographic and economic characteristics among migrants in respect of non-agricultural means of livelihood including self-employment, long-term urban residency interspersed with rural residency, offspring raised in urban settings even if selectively, not to mention any settlement inten-tion. More crucially, a new identity for migrants was needed to lay out policies in line with the vision of fulfilling the masses' needs. At stake in the symbolic construction of the migrant population was inequality in entitlements, especially those to publicly funded housing, healthcare, and education. Prior to 2011, only residents with local household registration

---

[30] That is, 流动人口 (liúdòng rénkǒu). Literally "flowing population". Visitors were distinguished from the transient population by drawing a line at the end of six months, after which they were regarded as ordinarily resident in a destination population management and statistical purposes by state organs concerned.

[31] That is, 外来务工人员 (wàilái wùgōng rényuán). Literally "personnel taking up employment who originate from elsewhere".

were eligible for these entitlements in the majority of urban settings. In order to symbolically usher in further reforms, policy-makers targeted a term already in popular use but unburdened by the legacy to be phased out, namely, *shimin*.[32] Literally "people of the city", the term *shimin* has been employed since 2014 in a series of neologisms in policy,[33] including *xinshimin*,[34] or "new citizen", and *shiminhua*,[35] literally "citizenisation". As the prospect of citizens gradually conferred entitlements by the state was arguably more congruent with official discourse than an underclass of internal migrants, the above neologisms and others were to be featured increasingly prominently in policy documents issued since 2011, which marked the commencement of the 12th Five-year Plan, and transition in party-state leadership from Hu Jintao to Xi Jinping. Key among these were the *Twelfth Five-year Plan* (National People's Congress, 2011), the *New-type Urbanisation Plan* (Central Committee of the Communist Party of China & State Council, 2014), *Opinions on Further Promoting Household Registration System Reform* (State Council, 2014b) and the Thirteenth Five-year Plan (National People's Congress, 2016). The import of these key policy statements was exemplified by, but not limited to, the symbolic erasure of the distinction between agricultural household registration and non-agricultural household registration in *Opinions on Further Promoting Household Registration System Reform*, as was done in Suzhou seven years earlier (see Municipality of Suzhou, 2007). In concert with this erasure, The *New-type Urbanisation Plan* repeatedly portrayed the barriers underlying the urban-rural dichotomy as structures to be progressively undone, thereby resolving the contradictions arising from various divisions between town and country.

[32] That is, "市民" (shìmín).

[33] Aside from usage in policy documents, the term "new citizen" and its variations were employed by officials such as the mayor of Hangzhou in Zhejiang province as early as 2008 (Shan, 2012). One of the earliest academic publications to refer to citizenisation was published in 2003 and cited 299 times (Y. Chen, 2003). A subsequent publication by the same author was cited 1027 times (Y. Chen, 2005).

[34] That is, "新市民" (xīnshìmín).

[35] That is, "市民化" (shìmínhuà).

2.5   Designing New Urban Citizenship

2.5.1   *Urban Residency, Settlement, and Transience*

By various means the population of China had been urbanising since the second half of the twentieth century. As a baseline estimate prior to land reform in the early 1950s, 10.6% of the population were living in urban areas in 1949 (Spence, 1990). By the start of the 2nd Five-year Plan in 1958, also the year marking the inception of contemporary household registration, this number had risen to 16.3%. And by the end of 1999 and 2009, the demographic urbanisation rate nearly doubled to 30.9 and 46.6% respectively (National Bureau of Statistics of the People's Republic of China, 2001, 2010). The *New-type Urbanisation Plan* set an even higher growth rate above six percentage points per decade, to an overall target of 60% of the total population ordinarily resident in urban areas by the end of 2020. This target was met earlier than planned by the end of 2019 with a demographic urbanisation rate of 60.6% (National Bureau of Statistics of the People's Republic of China, 2020). The *New-type Urbanisation Plan* also drew attention to the widening gap between the proportion of population ordinarily resident in urban areas in the nation overall, and the proportion of population registered as householders in the same urban locations they ordinarily resided in. The latter ratio, derived from the first, was said to be indicative of progress in citizenisation in respect of the portion of urban residents with access to public goods and services provided through urban jurisdictions. Urban residency was thus fractionalised into two categories, one for residents who were registered as local householders and therefore entitled to public goods and services, and another for non-local householders not entitled to these goods and services. In the year 2000, approximately 25% of the population were both local householders and urban residents, compared to 36.2% who were only urban residents, a difference of eleven percentage points. By 2012, this difference was enlarged to seventeen percentage points. With 44.4% of the population recorded as both local householders and urban residents by the end of 2019, the gap was narrowed by a mere one percentage point (National Bureau of Statistics of the People's Republic of China, 2020), and not the two percentage points anticipated for the shorter period between 2014 and 2020 in the *New-type Urbanisation Plan*. Nonetheless, it would appear that approximately 13 million people were made annually into so-called "new citizens" between 2016 and 2020 as aimed for in a series of high-level, closely co-ordinated acts of policy intervention (e.g. State Council, 2016b).

Even as the degree of permanent urban settlement rose to an unprecedented height of four in every ten persons by the end of 2019, other segments of the population of China were becoming or remaining transient. The latest census found 34.9% of the total population to be resident for more than six months in a location other than that of household registration by 1 November 2020 (Office of the Steering Group of the Seventh Census, 2021). A subset, or 26.6% of the total population, was resident for at least six months in a location within the jurisdiction of the same prefecture-level city but away from the location of household registration. Even after discounting this subset of short-distance and unsettled migrants, 8.3% of the population were still going about their lives far from their *de jure* addresses. When compared to figures from the census before last in 2010, this particular segment of the mobile population was increasing by an average of 19.3% annually, well above the overall population growth rate of 0.5% per year. In the calendar year of 2020, 20.2% of the total population were classified as migrant workers,[36] being those employed for six months or more away from the rural location of household registration, or those employed for six months or more in rural the location of household registration in a non-agricultural field of work (National Bureau of Statistics of the People's Republic of China, 2021). Among the 286 million or so migrant workers defined this way, 116 million were those employed in or near the location of household registration, while the other 170 million were earning their livelihood in locations beyond those of household registration.

2.5.2 The Regulation of Permanent Urban Settlement

Overall, the decade ending in 2020 was one of population redistribution into and between urban spaces. Both modes of urban residency, the one with local household registration status, and the one without, became more common. Growth in non-householder residents outpaced that in householder residents. In what ways were these demographic outcomes meant to be shaped by relevant policies issued since 2011? Specifically, how was permanent urban settlement regulated by different levels of

---

[36] Referred to using the familiar term *nongmingong* (农民工) in Chinese but simply dubbed 'migrant workers' in English instead of peasant-migrant workers.

government in the decade just past? The scaling of cities provided for by the 1954 Constitution that was operationalised in 1978 in terms of the size of the ordinarily resident population continued to play a prominent role in structuring urban settlement. Consistent with the political semiotics of preceding decades, the 1978 division between large, medium, and small cities was made even more delicate into one with five categories, each with a set of policy options which administrators of corresponding urban jurisdictions were eligible to employ in admitting new householder-residents. This demographic scale was constructed by splitting a city into its urban core and remaining areas before taking into account only the population ordinarily resident in the former (State Council, 2014a). In descending order, the scale was marked by the points 10, 5, 3, 0.5, and under 0.5 million residents ordinarily found in the urban core, corresponding respectively to "mega", "ultra-large", "large", "medium", and "small" cities (State Council, 2014a). Of these, "large" and "small" cities were sub-divided again in terms of the ordinarily resident population in the urban core. Controls permissible over the admittance of new citizens in "ultra-large cities" and "mega cities" were identical to each other in spite of their being on different points of the urban core population scale. Accordingly, "ultra-large cities" and "mega cities" were those in which expansion of permanent settlement was meant to be strictly limited. In less populated cities, any control from earlier policy periods such as purchase of residential property of a certain size in the locality was now deemed to be a barrier to population redistribution and would therefore have to be demolished or lowered in an orderly fashion. The only control small cities could exercise over potential new citizens was the requirement of a stable place of abode. In contrast, "ultra-large cities", "mega cities", and those "large cities" with 3 or more in the urban core were allowed to design and implement their own points-systems as a way of admitting new citizens on a selective basis. Unlike any earlier inbound migrant settlement programmes operated by some municipal authorities (L. Zhang, 2012), the current ones were made under the auspices of the 2014 national regulatory framework, and much more widespread across the nation (see Table 2.1).

The 2014 regulatory framework extended the logic of population distribution based on perceived and palpable disparities between cities. As such, it reinforced disparities arising from decades of policy-based fractionalisation of territory. It is doubtful if the framework was meant to result in distribution of population precisely in proportion to land

Table 2.1 Controls municipal governments are permitted to exercise over the admittance of new household registrants since 2014

Urban core population scale	Population of core urban area	Place-of-abode requirements	Participation in the social insurance programme	Points-system	Additional requirements
Mega	Over 10 million	Yes	Yes	Yes	Not mentioned
Ultra-large	Over 5 million	Yes	Yes	Yes	Not mentioned
Large	Between 1 and 3 million; between 3 and 5 million	Yes	Yes, but for a period of no longer than 5 years	Yes if the population exceeds 3 million	Yes
Medium	Between 0.5 and 1 million in core urban areas	Yes	Yes, but for a period of no longer than 3 years	No	Yes, but may not include the size of the place of abode or its market value
Small	Under 0.5 million	Yes	No	No	No

Sources National People's Congress (2016) and State Council (2014b, 2016b)

area and production capacity. On the contrary, the framework paved the way for a complex and unpredictable pricing system composed of markets operated by municipal authorities under the oversight of the central government. In this system, cities, just like migrants seeking to settle or otherwise live in them, could be priced differentially, meaning massive potential for the creation of surplus value through economic transactions. Any attempt by populous municipalities in setting their own prices for householder-residency through inbound migration settlement programmes must be seen in light of further policy interventions crafted at the central level by top-level designers, and of alternative pathways to betterment available to internal migrants.

Indeed, interventions from central policy-makers informed by high-level design were already forthcoming to allay municipal authorities' concerns with the fiscal burden associated with settling additional householder-residents. Acknowledgement of inadequate central support in the *Thirteenth Five-year Plan* (National People's Congress, 2016) was accompanied by clarification of fiscal costs and benefits for municipalities "absorbing" internal migrants in *Opinions on Further Progressing New-Type Urbanization* (State Council, 2016c). These clarifications established more explicitly than ever before the principle of proportionality, whereby fiscal funds from higher-level authorities would be provided in proportion to the number of additional new citizens accepted within the 2014 regulatory framework. Similarly, *Notice Regarding Fiscal Policies Designed to Support the Citizenisation of the Rural Migrant Population* (State Council, 2016a) outlined performance criteria deserving of central fiscal support apart from the number of additional new citizens admitted. Another document made known other criteria such as public expenditure per capita, fiscal status, and effectiveness in implementation at the local level (Ministry of Finance, 2016). By policy then, greater fiscal rewards would be available to local authorities with a speedier policy response within the 2014 regulatory framework, greater number of migrants settled permanently through citizenisation, and higher average expenditure in the process. In order to further stimulate the market for internal migrant resettlement, a subsequent centrally issued policy document specifically encouraged points-systems operating at the sub-municipal, that is district level, to be created in ultra-large cities and mega-cities (National Development and Reform Commission, 2018). While points-systems have not further proliferated as a result, policy developments since 2014 act as a potent reminder to examine fractions of jurisdiction seemingly too small to matter to statecraft, and yet in which statecraft is subtly manifest. Just as cities have between them socio-economic gradients down which migrants may move, the same logic could well be applied to urban districts within the same city. In respect of intra-urban disparity of state provisions for resettling migrants, it would be pertinent to note that the registration of householders in urban China at the level of sub-district entities known as "street offices", and the public service implications of such a delicate political geography (Xiang Wang, 2020).

Socio-economic disparity between and within cities leaves internal migrants with options which vary in viability. Internal migrants could return to and remain in the place of household registration, making use of land-use entitlements in rural areas as the means of livelihood (Q. X. Wang & Zhang, 2017). Alternatively, as 298 million people did in 2014,[37] they could opt for transience, presumably taking advantage of higher wage levels in *de facto* places of residence, minimising costs incurred during income generation, and relocating again as market conditions changed. Compared to returning home and remaining transient, resettling would mean a considerable investment of household resources in an urban destination exemplified by the purchase of residential property in an urban district, a focal point of the 2014 regulatory framework. Such a major investment may motivate or demotivate migrant resettlement in a specific urban district, or more generally in a particular municipality. Investments like this would effectively mean rejection of most other urban locales for resettlement purposes. Apparently, the challenges of committing to one single urban locale did not prevent an average of 13 million people from completing such a journey towards resettlement annually between 2016 and 2020. More than ever before, municipal authorities in China found themselves in the nexus adjoining state attempts in redistributing a mobile population and responses to these attempts by a migrant population willing to engage in different kinds of residency arrangement.

2.5.3 New Citizenship in Beijing and Suzhou

The 2014 national regulatory framework permitted mega cities like Beijing and ultra-large cities like Suzhou to each design its own points-systems, meaning a considerable amount of latitude in adjusting the strictness of controls over permanent migrant settlement. As a mega city, Beijing could legitimately erect higher barriers for prospective new citizens than Suzhou, making the policies issued by the former a basis of comparison with those of the latter.[38] In order to place barriers in local policies in context, major indicators in respect of urbanisation from key

---

[37] Or 21.8%, computed with figures from China Statistical Yearbook 2015 http://www.stats.gov.cn/tjsj/ndsj/2015/indexeh.htm.

[38] By some accounts Suzhou is only a large city and not an ultra-large city as per the terminology of *Notice Regarding Adjustments to the Classification of Urban Scale* (2014b). Differences in reckoning was possible due to the operationalisation of the term "urban core" by government agencies with contrasting reporting practices, and to changes in boundaries separating administrative divisions. In spite of such complications, what remains valid is the relative ranking of Suzhou as lower than Beijing on the 2014 demographic scale. The precedent in retrospective clarification of urban scale in the case of Suzhou back in 1993 already noted in Sect. 2.3.2 suggests a recurrence of the same in the future.

points in time are shown in Table 2.2. Whereas the proportion of residents on land in cities indicates the gross demographic urbanisation rate, the proportion of non-householder residents on land in cities represents the notional extent of citizen-making still to be realised. Targets set for the year 2020 by state policy were at least 60% for the former and no more than 55% for the latter.

Judging by the above indicators, the 2020 gross urbanisation target set by the central government was more than achieved by both Suzhou and Beijing as early as 2010, one year before the policy period in question. In terms of gross demographic urbanisation, the two municipalities had been performing above the national average since, an observation consistent with both being among top ten destinations for internal migration (Department of Service & Management of Migrant Population of the National Health & Family Planning Commission of China, 2015). On the other hand, in terms of the settlement of migrants and the conferring of public service entitlements, Suzhou did appear to be behind Beijing and the nation by the end of 2020. From this limited point of view alone, Suzhou could be expected to respond to the central government by issuing policies with lower barriers when compared to Beijing. In several

Table 2.2 Major indicators of urbanisation between 2010 and 2020 in Beijing and Suzhou

Residential category as a proportion of the population	National (%)	Beijing (%)	Suzhou (%)
The year ending 2010			
• Residents on land in cities	49.8	86.0	70.1
• Non-householder residents on land in cities	19.5	35.9	51.0
The year ending 2014			
• Residents on land in cities	54.8	86.4	79.9
• Non-householder residents on land in cities	21.8	38.1	38.4
The year ending 2020			
• Residents on land in cities	63.9	87.5	100
• Non-householder residents on land in cities	34.9	38.5	61.4

Compiled and derived from figures available from publications by the National Bureau of Statistics and its local counterparts. Figures for Suzhou exclude the population of county-level cities under Suzhou's administration important respects, nonetheless, policies in Suzhou did not turn out as expected in terms of their form and function despite similarity of rhetoric (Cheung, 2021).

The desire to achieve targets set by the central government notwithstanding, points-systems were meant to provide each relevant local authority with the means of varying the extent and speed of citizenisation in support of local developmental needs (Central Committee of the Communist Party of China & State Council, 2014). Accordingly, each of these local authorities devised their own series of applicant eligibility criteria plus selection criteria, and structured them in a way deemed suitable. Local policy form was modified by altering the number of criteria as well as the criteria themselves. In each points-system, applicants would be scored and ranked according to the extent to which they met the criteria set by local authorities. Successful applicants were those able to accumulate points above a threshold set by local authorities. Any institutional barriers preventing settlement at the local level prior to 2014 were thereby replaced with a combination of institutional and socio-economic barriers by which local householders-to-be were differentiated from those other applicants who would remain non-householder residents, at least for the time being. In this way, Suzhou's points-system made 2640 local residents into new-citizens-to-be in 2018, compared to the 6019 additions to the household register through the Beijing points-system.

The Suzhou points-system was structured by the balance of "basic points", "additions", and "deductions" covering different sets of selection criteria (Municipality of Suzhou, 2015a, 2015b). The basic-and-non-basic structure was also found in the consultation draft outlining the Beijing points-system (Municipality of Beijing, 2015), but eventually removed from the one meant for trial implementation (Municipality of Beijing, 2016) and from the current version (Municipality of Beijing, 2020a, 2020b). Ever since the consultation draft, deductions in Beijing were embedded within each set of stated selection criteria. A rather straightforward criterion in terms of policy form was the highest educational qualification attained by the applicant, which in both municipalities was positively scored without deductions of any kind. Points were available for applicants with junior college degrees or above in Suzhou, and undergraduate degrees or above in Beijing. In both systems, scoring was progressive with the degree of attainment. Applicants with lower qualifications or no qualifications were not penalised, but would nonetheless be less competitive in this specific respect. And in this particular respect, local policy form showed convergence towards the standard set by the central government. Convergence in local policy function could be observed here as the criterion that was employed to achieve the same end of selecting relatively more educated applicants.

Like educational attainment, the lifespan was fractionalised and scored differentially, but with greater divergence in form between the two municipalities. Applicant age between 18 and 40 was positively scored in Suzhou under "basic points", but not age in higher brackets. Age under 45 was originally an eligibility criterion in the 2015 consultation draft concerning Beijing with no scoring associated with it. This eligibility criterion was relaxed to just below retirement age (50 for women, 60 for men) in the version for trial implementation in 2016, with a selection criterion added where 20 points were awarded to applicants for being under the age of 45. The scoring by this criterion was almost exactly in the same form as in the system in Suzhou. By 2020, however, positive scoring in Beijing took the regressive form for those under the age of 49. Age under 45 attracted 20 points; under 46, 16 points; under 47, 12 points, and so forth. No points were available for age 49 or above. The delicate fractions near the retirement age were presented by the city's chief policy-making body as a deliberate attempt to encourage those still in the work force to settle down permanently (Beijing Municipal Commission of Development & Reform, 2020).

Local barriers did not always conform to the structure specified by the central government, however. Divergence of form was especially notable in local authorities' inclusion of demerit points targeting presumably undesirable socio-demographic and socio-economic attributes. In Suzhou, deductions were applicable to applicants with a criminal record in the previous five years, with 200 points taken away for each infraction. Lesser deductions ranging from 30 to 50 points were applicable for each fraudulent act which contravened neither administrative nor criminal law. Further, breach of family planning regulations in aid of others formed its own deduction category, with the performance of illegal pregnancy termination or medically unnecessary gender determination procedures attracting a deduction of 50 points. In Beijing, any criminal record would render a resident ineligible for new citizenship application. On the other hand, each count of administrative detention in the previous five years would mean a deduction of 30 points. Within the same time-frame, each tax-related breach would result in a deduction of 12 points. Hence apart from the central government there was also divergence of policy form between the two municipalities in respect of deductions.

Within their respective jurisdictions, it was clear that local authorities in Suzhou and Beijing employed symbolic means apart from fractionalisation in response to the central government's calls to enhance demographic urbanisation. The form specified by the central government, namely, that of qualification, underwent partial inversion in both municipalities to also include disqualification. That non-householder residents would qualify to different degrees as new citizens were already clear enough in national policy; local policy responses constructed the converse, that the same people could potentially be unsuitable to different degrees. Another very significant inversion was the purchase of local residential property, which the central government explicitly ruled out as a pre-requisite for settlement in large, medium, and small cities (State Council, 2016b). Local residential property purchase became symbolically inverted from a barrier into a positively scored selection criterion in Suzhou in spite of its ultra-large city status (Cheung, 2021). In other words, although property purchase could have been made into an eligibility criterion in Suzhou without divergence from central policy, it was made instead into an incentive for potential new citizens. Purchase of each residential property measuring 75 m^2 or above was awarded 60 points, with a progressive increment of 20 extra points for properties measuring 100 m^2, 125 m^2, 150 m^2 and so forth (Municipality of Suzhou, 2015b). The maximum number of points to be accumulated through property purchase was capped at 200. In contrast, proof of continuous rental of residential property could result in no more than 50 points in total. Although not in the form of a requirement, the criterion gave preference overwhelmingly to property owners over those who had chosen not to or were unable to acquire property in Suzhou at the time of application. Except for recognition of multiple residential properties, the purchasing criterion remained largely unchanged in the points-system revised a month before the end of the policy period in question (Municipality of Suzhou, 2020a, 2020b). In fact, the gain in points associated with a purchased property of 75 m^2 over those with continuous rental payments was even greater than in 2015. In Beijing, on the other hand, a mere half-point advantage was conferred upon property owners compared to tenants, with points accumulating this way for every year of local residence (Municipality of Beijing, 2020b). In respect of accommodation, therefore, inverted barriers set up through the points-system were considerably lower in Beijing than in Suzhou. This urban-urban disparity was not in the direction expected in view of the

2014 national regulatory framework, nor was the smaller scale of permanent settlement of migrants in Suzhou in the few years before 2021. Intra-urban disparities within the urban core of Suzhou will be pursued in connection with public service entitlements in Chapter 3.

2.6   Policy, Poleis, and Disparity

The current chapter presented a number of symbolic loci, processes, and means through which Chinese state policies brought into being urban spaces and urban populations in the years leading to 2020. Rather than acting like a sieve, however, policy did not uniformly desiccate the nation's already uneven geography or demography. Instead, it created new boundaries with reimagined urban district designations based on the Constitution, a refined urban scale based on population size in urban districts, and diversified inbound urban migration programmes into urban districts based on profiling. These policy moves were layered in such a way as to redistribute the national population across three main types of urban residency arrangement: permanence, resettlement, and transience. Remarkably, the preponderance of transience was still increasing even as the state called for, and apparently succeeded in, admitting 100 million urban residents as householders registered at the sub-district level across urban municipalities in the nation. Local policy, while often taking on the form of national policy aimed at promoting citizenisation, did not always serve the function of lowering barriers that prevented local household registration. Such a homologous relationship between sets of policy was especially salient in the above examination of the points-system designed by the Municipality of Suzhou, and the inverted barrier of local residential property purchase featured within it. And when applicant profiling in Suzhou and Beijing was compared, a hemilogous relationship emerged. In other words, pre-requisites for household registration had become even more specific to individual urban locations than in previous policy cycles.

Inter-urban disparities in recent policy in the domain of household registration made rather prominent relations of exchange between the central government and local authorities on the one hand, and between both and the citizenry on the other. The central government, which had set its sights on lifting the rate of citizenisation, was prepared to offer fiscal stimulus to local authorities for admitting as householders those urban residents willing to invest their own household resources into this kind of resettlement. Local authorities, who stood to benefit from both central funding and population-driven growth, had to decide which of their non-householder residents to settle down, and which ones to retain as a migrant labour force. Already transient, the latter group of urban residents faced choices between urban settlement destinations, each with its own demands and offers in the name of household registration. For internal migrants, the system of incentives and disincentives laid down in multiple layers of policy had become so intricate that no single residency arrangement and no single urban location was overwhelmingly advantageous over all others. If state policy had ever made a handful of cities ideal to live in, this was no longer the case by the end of 2020. Neither straightforwardly better nor worse in relation to each other, cities became different urban spaces which urban-bound internal migrants themselves needed to distinguish between in terms of their own preferences, even as distinctions were applied to them by local authorities under the influence of the central government.

References

Adam, C., Hurka, S., Knill, C., & Steinebach, Y. (2019). *Policy accumulation and the democratic responsiveness trap*. Cambridge University Press.

Beijing Municipal Commission of Development & Reform. (2020). *Outcomes of the public consultation concerning "Measures of Managing the New Citizenship Points-system in Beijing"*. http://fgw.beijing.gov.cn/zmhd/dczj/202007/t20200716_1950456.htm

Béland, D. (2007). Ideas and institutional change in social security: Conversion, layering, and policy drift. *Social Science Quarterly, 88*(1), 20–38. https://doi.org/10.1111/j.1540-6237.2007.00444.x

Campbell, J. L. (2002). Ideas, politics, and public policy. *Annual Review of Sociology, 28*, 21–38. https://doi.org/10.1146/annurev.soc.28.110601.141111

Carter, P. (2012). Policy as palimpsest. *Policy and Politics, 40*(3), 423–443. https://doi.org/10.1332/030557312x626613

Cartier, C., & Hu, D. (2020). Suzhou and the city-region: The administrative divisions in historical perspective and rural-urban transition. In B. Tang & P. Cheung (Eds.), *Suzhou in transition: Social change and development in contemporary China* (pp. 193–213). Routledge.

Central Committee of the Communist Party of China. (2013). *Pedagogical outline of the scientific outlook on development*. Xuexi Press, People's Press.

Central Committee of the Communist Party of China, & State Council (2014). *National new-type urbanisation plan (2014–2020)*. The People's Press.

Chan, K. W., & Buckingham, W. (2008). Is China abolishing the Hukou system? *The China Quarterly*(195), 582–606.

Chen, Y. (2003). The citizenization of farmers of land requisition. *Journal of East China Normal University, 35*(03), 88–95,124.

Chen, Y. (2005). "Peasant-labor": System and identity. *Sociological Studies*, (03), 119–132, 244.

Cheung, P. (2021). Location-specific citizenship: State visions of spatial selectivity in the cities of Beijing and Suzhou. *Territory, Politics, Governance.* https://doi.org/10.1080/21622671.2021.1982760

Department of Service and Management of Migrant Population of the National Health and Family Planning Commission of China. (2015). Research report on migrant population trend and policy considerations in the period of the 13th Five-year Plan. *2015 Report on China's Migrant Population Development* (pp. 3–17). China Population Publishing House.

Fei, X. (1939). *Peasant life in China.* Kegan Paul, Trench, Trubner and Co., Ltd.

Foucault, M. (1971/1972). *The archaeology of knowledge and the discourse on language* (A. M. Sheridan Smith, Trans.). Pantheon Books.

Gal, S. (2016). Scale-making: Comparison and perspective as ideological projects. In E. Summerson Carr & M. Lempert (Eds.), *Scale: Discourse and dimensions of social life* (pp. 91–111). University of California Press.

Gal, S., & Irvine, J. T. (2019). *Signs of difference.* Cambridge University Press.

Habermas, J. (1981/2007). *The theory of communicative action—Two: Lifeworld and system* (T. McCarthy, Trans.). Beacon Press.

Hacker, J. S. (2004). Privatizing risk without privatizing the welfare state: The hidden politics of social policy retrenchment in the United States. *American Political Science Review, 98*(2), 243–260. https://doi.org/10.1017/s0003055404001121

Hall, P. A. (1993). Policy paradigms, social-learning, and the state—The case of economic policy-making in Britain. *Comparative Politics, 25*(3), 275–296. https://doi.org/10.2307/422246

Ho, P. (2006). *Institutions in transition.* Oxford University Press.

Huang, S. (2013). The evolution of policies for China's migrant workers since 1978. In J. Pan & H. Wei (Eds.), *Annual report on urban development of China* (pp. 78–95). Social Sciences Academic Press.

Jin, S. (2015). *The policy research on the path of the citizenization of peasant-workers.* China Development Press.

Karatani, K., & Lippit, S. M. (2004/2012). *History and repetition.* Columbia University Press.

King, R. (1977). Land Reform: A world survey (pp. 79–106). Bell.

Lefebvre, H. (1974/1991). *The production of space* (D. Nicholson-Smith, Trans.). Blackwell.

Li, L. (2020). Junxian is basis of the Chinese institutional framework. *Historical Review*(04), 30–35.

Luhmann, N., Kastner, F., & Schiff, D. (Eds.). (1993/2009). *Law as a social system*. Oxford University Press.

Ma, L. J. C. (2005). Urban administrative restructuring, changing scale relations and local economic development in China. *Political Geography, 24*(4), 477–497.

Mandelbrot, B. B. (1983). *The fractal geometry of nature*. W.H. Freeman and Company.

Mandelbrot, B. B., Berger, J. M., Kahane, J. P., & Peyriere, J. (Eds.). (2013). *Multifractals and 1/f noise: Wild self-affinity in physics (1963–1976)*. Springer.

Marx, K. (1976). *Capital: A critique of political economy Volume I* (B. Fowkes, Trans.). Penguin Books.

Mettler, S. (2016). The policyscape and the challenges of contemporary politics to policy maintenance. *Perspectives on Politics, 14*(2), 369–390. https://doi.org/10.1017/s1537592716000074

Ministry of Finance. (2016). *Notice regarding the regulation of financial incentives for the citizenisation of rural migrant population* (Caiyu (2016) Number 162). http://yss.mof.gov.cn/ybxzyzf/jhxzyzf/201612/t20161205_2472991.html

Municipality of Beijing. (2015). *Means of managaging the new citizenship points-system in Beijing* (Consultation Draft). http://www.beijing.gov.cn/sqmy/sqmysy/wqzjdc/t1413973.htm

Municipality of Beijing. (2016). *Notice concerning the means of managaging the new citizenship points-system in Beijing* (Trial Version) (Jingzhenbanfa 2016 Number 39). http://www.beijing.gov.cn/zhengce/zhengcefagui/201905/t20190522_59544.html

Municipality of Beijing. (2020a). *Notice concerning details of the operational management of the new citizenship points-system in Beijing* (Jingrenshekaifafa 2020 Number 8). http://www.beijing.gov.cn/zhengce/zhengcefagui/202007/t2020a0716_1950475.html

Municipality of Beijing. (2020b). *Notice concerning the issuing of measures of managing the new citizenship points-system in Beijing* (Jingzhengbanfa 2020 Number 9). http://www.beijing.gov.cn/zhengce/zhengcefagui/rmzc/202007/t2020b0716_1950304.html

Municipality of Suzhou. (2007). *Temporary measures for the registration of householders-to-be* (Revised) (Sufu 2007 Number 124). http://www.zfxxgk.suzhou.gov.cn/sjjg/szsrlzyhshbzj/szsrcfwzx/201212/t20121203_179453.html

Municipality of Suzhou. (2015a). *Means of managing the points-system for the transient population* (Sufuguizi 2015 Number 6). http://www.zfxxgk.suzhou.gov.cn/sxqzf/szsrmzf/2015a12/t2015a1214_654708.html

Municipality of Suzhou. (2015b). *Scoring criteria of the points-system for the transient population* (Sufuguizi 2015 Number 7). http://www.zfxxgk.suzhou.gov.cn/sjjg/szszffzbgs/201601/t20160118_668648.html

Municipality of Suzhou. (2020a). *Means of managing the points-system for the transient population* (Sufuguizi 2020 Number 15). https://www.suzhou.gov.cn/szsrmzf/zfwj/2020a11/53f6b237c13f4bf1b09df5accd14053d.shtml

Municipality of Suzhou. (2020b). *Scoring criteria of the points-system for the transient population* (Sufuguizi 2020 Number 16). https://www.suzhou.gov.cn/szsrmzf/zfwj/2020b11/5f567825d58d48ed8e3353f971bff6c5.shtml

National Bureau of Statistics of the People's Republic of China. (2001). *Statistical Communiqué of the People's Republic of China on the 1999 National Economic and Social Development*. http://www.stats.gov.cn/tjsj/tjgb/ndtjgb/qgndtjgb/200203/t20020331_30013.html

National Bureau of Statistics of the People's Republic of China. (2010). *Statistical Communiqué of the People's Republic of China on the 2009 National Economic and Social Development*. http://www.stats.gov.cn/tjsj/tjgb/ndtjgb/qgndtjgb/201002/t20100225_30024.html

National Bureau of Statistics of the People's Republic of China. (2020). *Statistical Communiqué of the People's Republic of China on the 2019 National Economic and Social Development*. http://www.stats.gov.cn/tjsj/zxfb/202002/t20200228_1728913.html

National Bureau of Statistics of the People's Republic of China. (2021). *Statistical Communiqué of the People's Republic of China on the 2020 National Economic and Social Development*. http://www.stats.gov.cn/english/PressRelease/202102/t20210228_1814177.html

National Development and Reform Commission. (2018). *Notice concerning key tasks in the implementation of new-type urbanization in 2018*. http://www.gov.cn/xinwen/2018-03/13/content_5273637.htm

National People's Congress. (1958). *Regulation of household registration*. http://www.npc.gov.cn/wxzl/gongbao/2000-12/10/content_5004332.htm

National People's Congress. (1959). *Decision concerning the leadership of counties by cities*. http://www.npc.gov.cn/wxzl/gongbao/2000-12/10/content_5004348

National People's Congress. (1982). *Constitution of the People's Republic of China*. http://www.npc.gov.cn/wxzl/wxzl/2000-12/06/content_4421.htm

National People's Congress. (1993). *Amendments to the Constitution of the People's Republic of China*. http://www.npc.gov.cn/wxzl/wxzl/2000-12/05/content_4585.htm

National People's Congress. (2011). *Outline of The Twelfth Five-year Plan of the Economy and Society of the People's Republic of China*. http://www.gov.cn/2011lh/content_1825838.htm

National People's Congress. (2016). *Outline of The Thirteenth Five-year Plan of the Economy and Society of the People's Republic of China*. http://paper.peo ple.com.cn/rmrb/html/2016-03/18/nw.D110000renmrb_20160318_1-01. htm

National People's Congress. (2018). *Constitution of the People's Republic of China*. http://www.npc.gov.cn/englishnpc/constitution2019/201911/1f65146fb6104dd3a2793875d19b5b29.shtml

National People's Congress. (2019a). *Land administration law of the People's Republic of China*. http://www.npc.gov.cn/npc/c30834/2019a09/d1e6c1 a1eec345eba23796c6e8473347.shtml

National People's Congress. (2019b). *Urban Real estate administration law of the People's Republic of China*. http://www.npc.gov.cn/npc/c30834/201 9b09/54daabc2a4014a3f8d3097bfaaf88f96.shtml

Office of the Steering Group of the Seventh Census. (2021). *Major figures on 2020 population census of China*. http://www.stats.gov.cn/tjsj/pcsj/rkpc/d7c/202111/P020211126523667366751.pdf

Owen, R., & White Cooper, W. (1843). *Lectures on the comparative anatomy and physiology of the invertebrate animals*. Longman, Brown, Green and Longmans.

Pieke, F. (2009). The politics of rural land use planning. In P. Ho (Ed.), *Developmental dilemmas* (pp. 79–106). Routledge.

Rosenfeld, V. R., & Nordahl, T. E. (2016). Semigroup theory of symmetry. *Journal of Mathematical Chemistry, 54*(9), 1758–1776. https://doi.org/10.1007/s10910-016-0653-4

Sahlins, M. D. (1976). *Culture and practical reason*. University of Chicago Press.

Shan, J. (2012). *The study of citizenization of Chinese migrant workers*. Social Sciences Academic Press.

Shang Yang. (1928). *The book of Lord Shang* (J. J. Duyvendak, Trans.). Probsthain.

Shang Yang. (2017). *The book of Lord Shang* (Y. Pines, Trans.). Columbia University Press.

Spence, J. D. (1990). *The search for modern China*. Norton.

State Council. (1981). *Notice concerning the strict control of rural labour from entry to cities and of the conversion of agricultural population into non-agricultural population*. https://law.lawtime.cn/d562210567304.html

State Council. (1985). *Provisions on the administration of administrative divisions*. http://www.gov.cn/test/2009-03/30/content_1272329.htm

State Council. (1986). *Notice concerning the approval of The Report on City Establishment and City Leadership of Counties*. http://www.gov.cn/zhengce/content/2012-08/20/content_7186.htm

State Council. (1993). *Concerning the approval of larger-city status for Suzhou and Xuzhou*. http://www.law-lib.com/law/law_view.asp?id=303816

State Council. (2014a). *Notice regarding adjustments to the classification of urban scale* (Guofa (2014) Number 51). http://www.gov.cn/zhengce/content/201411/20/content_9225.htm

State Council. (2014b). *Opinions on further promoting household registration system reform* (Guofa (2014) Number 25). http://www.gov.cn/zhengce/content/2014-07/30/content_8944.htm

State Council. (2016a). *Notice regarding fiscal policies designed to support the citizenisation of the rural migrant population* (Guofa (2016) Number 44). http://www.gov.cn/zhengce/content/2016-08/05/content_5097845.htm

State Council. (2016b). *Notice regarding the proposal to promote the transfer of household registration of 100 million people* (Guofa (2016) Number 72). http://www.gov.cn/zhengce/content/2016-10/11/content_5117442.htm

State Council. (2016c). *Opinions on further progressing new-type urbanization* (Guofa (2016) Number 8). http://www.gov.cn/zhengce/content/2016-02/06/content_5039947.htm

State Council. (2021). *Regulation on the implementation of the land administration law of the People's Republic of China* (Guoling Number 743). http://www.gov.cn/zhengce/content/2021-07/30/content_5628461.htm

The Editors of Xinhuanet. (2011). "Top-level design": New political jargon hints at the future of China's reforms. *Xinhuanet.* http://news.xinhuanet.com/politics/2011lh/2011-03/13/c_121181278

Thelen, K. (2004). *How institutions evolve: The political economy of skills in Germany, Britain, the United States, and Japan.* Cambridge University Press.

Wallace, J. L. (2014). *Cities and stability.* Oxford Univeristy Press.

Wang, Q. X., & Zhang, X. L. (2017). Three rights separation: China's proposed rural land rights reform and four types of local trials. *Land Use Policy, 63,* 111–121. https://doi.org/10.1016/j.landusepol.2017.01.027

Wang, X. (2020). Permits, points, and permanent household registration: recalibrating Hukou Policy under "Top-Level Design." *Journal of Current Chinese Affairs, 49*(3), 269–290. https://doi.org/10.1177/1868102619894739

Young, J. (2013). *China's Hukou system.* Palgrave Macmlllan.

Zhang, L. (2012). Economic migration and urban citizenship in China: The role of points systems. *Population and Development Review, 38*(3), 503–+.https://doi.org/10.1111/j.1728-4457.2012.00514.x

Zhou, T. (2014). The institutional shift from "city-leading-counties" to "province-leading counties". *Chinese Cadres Tribune* (07), 7–11. https://doi.org/10.14117/j.cnki.cn11-3331/d.2014.07.016

CHAPTER 3

Urban Classes

Abstract This chapter addresses the ways in which the Chinese state's policies in population management deal with inequality in public service provision in urban settings. In seeking to go beyond the appeal to class and space, it makes a number of conceptual connections between equality, freedom, and rule. It also identifies the parties to exchange as being more than simply the undifferentiated state and a similarly undifferentiated society. The three paradigmatic perspectives from the introductory chapter are again put to use with the benefit of such elaborations in the examination of policies which allow internal migrants without local household registration to access publicly funded education for their children. Unexpected variations in policy within the Municipality of Suzhou are discussed in terms of freedom *in* trading with the state as opposed to freedom *from* trading with the state in return for public service provision. In spite of state policy and also because of it, inequality in public service provision is shown to be far more complex than previously thought.

Keywords Agency · Class · Education · Public service provision · Suzhou

© The Author(s), under exclusive license to Springer Nature
Singapore Pte Ltd. 2022
P. Cheung, *Statecraft in Symbols*,
https://doi.org/10.1007/978-981-19-3319-6_3

...in a country that has the true way, order does not depend on the prince, and the people do not merely follow the officials. (Shang Yang, 1928, p. 214)

THE question, which is the better man, is determinable only in the estate of government and policy, though it be mistaken for a question of nature... (Hobbes, 1675, p. 68)

...I desire neither to rule nor to be ruled; but if I waive my claim to be king, I make this condition, that neither I nor any of my posterity shall be subject to any one of you. (attributed to Otanes, Herodotus, 1921, p. 111)

3.1   ORIENTATION

In the decade ending 2020, a raft of policy coincided with sustained increases to the urban population in China, including the fraction which became known as new citizens in state-sponsored discourse. As shown in the previous chapter, the central government and local authorities made provisions for these urban residents to enjoy the same entitlements to local public goods and services as those who were much more established as registered local householders. In conformity with policies issued at different levels of administration, such programmes of citizenisation have been highly selective. Instead of leaving the majority of non-householder urban residents to live in systemic inequality, however, policy from the same period also featured the broader objective of "basic public-service entitlement equalisation".[1] How would the rhetoric of entitlement equalisation be realised in policy form and policy function down the administrative hierarchy, especially when one recalls the teleological gradualism in *The Scientific Outlook on Development* (see Sect. 2.4.1)? It is such rhetoric, and its realisation which the current chapter reports on. The chapter again focuses on the Municipality of Suzhou and how its equalisation policies compare with those of the provincial and central governments. Intra-urban comparison in policy is presented below to reveal additional governance dynamics at play in demographic urbanisation in the decade leading up to 2021, dynamics to be shown to depend on even more intricately inter-connected fractionalisation of territory and

---

[1] That is, 公共服务均等化 (gōnggòng fúwù jūnděnghuà).

population. Such comparison will be made with reference to the District of Wujiang, which as a result of its former status as a county-level city was able to issue its own policies covering both citizenisation and entitlement equalisation despite having been a constituent of Suzhou's urban core since 2012. As shall be shown throughout the chapter, lines of policy-conferred privilege are drawn across the population in ways far more complex than recognised in existing research.

3.2 INEQUALITY AMONG URBAN RESIDENTS

3.2.1 Empirical Perspectives

Among existing research one can think for example of Xueguang Zhou's (2004) study of state-level politics and the resultant impact upon social stratification and mobility among urbanites in the first 45 years of the People's Republic of China. Tony Saich's (2008) analysis of state welfare policies stretched from the same starting point, passing through the beginning of the reform and opening up period, commonly marked as 1979, through to the early years following coming into effect of policies undergirding the Minimum Living Standard Scheme in 2001. David Goodman's (2014) study of the middle class in urban China up to the beginning of the presidency of Xi Jinping was thrown against the sharp relief of shifting ideological underpinnings of discourse sponsored by the Party. These studies, while clearly acknowledging the importance of internal migrants in examining inequality, were focused upon established urban residents, that is, householders already entitled to basic public goods and services. Research more directly concerned with state policy towards internal migrants was exemplified by that of Dorothy Solinger, whose repertoire pointed to comprehensively engineered exclusion of rural-to-urban migrants in urban life, dubbed the "urban underclass", both prior to the policy debut of the notion of minimum living standard (1993, 1999) and after (2006), but before those of citizenisation and entitlement equalisation. To these investigations of social strata, Carolyn Cartier, Hu De, and Lawrence Ma added theirs on the administrative division of land in the opening up and reform era (Cartier & Hu, 2020; Ma, 2005). How policy conflates social and geographical distinctions among the populace is not yet well understood, though with regard to local citizenisation efforts recent studies have begun to shed light on their design (Cheung, 2021; Wang, 2020). To the extent that distinctions mean inequality, inequality has under recent policy become more localised than ever before, raising doubts over any notion of geographical invariance of social strata.

3.2.2   Theoretical Perspectives

Fine-grained policy-induced inequality requires further theoretical examination through the paradigmatic perspectives introduced in Chapter 1. This is partly because class and space, as conceptual lenses typically relied upon in previous studies, tend to permit only views of the population and territory as large fractions. As already shown in relation to citizenisation policies in Chapter 2, however, both land and people in China are subject to minute fractionalisation down to the sub-district level in urban settings. Paradigmatically, minute fractionalisation by policy can be equated to variation in the incursion of system into lifeworld. System desiccates lifeworld not only through variations in policy form, function, and rhetoric, but also in the very design of bureaucracy itself as criss-crossing lines of governance prerogatives. From this perspective, parties to exchange in the market for internal migrant resettlement are not simply state and society, but rather sub-divisions of each. Accordingly, the agency of each party to exchange and their relations to each other need to be accounted for. In allowing inter-agentive relations to be more theoretically salient, the heterogeneity of inequality comes into view. In this regard, multiplicity in the modes of exchange (see Sect. 1.2.3) is an important theoretical point departure for the current chapter. As a theoretical extension, the four main modes of exchange observable in the realm of geopolitics are assumed to be the sublation of corresponding modes of exchange operating on smaller scales. Each mode of exchange would then be typified by a different variety of unequal inter-agentive relations between a different set of parties to exchange. These concepts are developed below to facilitate the analysis of policy to follow.

3.2.3   Equality Before Law and Policy

In the absence of a unitary social contract then, is the notion of equality merely a hyperbole? Shang Yang's espousal of equality before the law, somewhat like Hobbes' insistence of endowed equality among humans, was meant to consolidate state power by minimising inherited privilege. Nonetheless Hobbes, just like Shang Yang, did not shy away from instilling inequality by means of law and policy. In yet another historical context, but also one where rulership came under scrutiny, Otanes was reported to have championed *isonomin* (ἰσονομίην) to counter the institution of monarchy in Persia (see Herodotus, 1921, 1998, 2005). Rendered into "Equality" (Herodotus, 2005, p. 115) or "multitude's rule" (Herodotus, 1921, p. 107), the term *isonomin* also carried the sense of equal distribution and that of equilibrium. In Herodotus' account, Otanes failed to convince other members of nobility to support such a form of rule, withdrew from the ensuing leadership race, and made the declaration concerning freedom from rule quoted at the beginning of the current chapter. Herodotus (2005, p. 111) inserted commentary at this point of the narrative, observing that:

> *Otanes took no part in the contest but stood aside; and to this day his house (and none other in Persia) remains free, nor is compelled to render any unwilling obedience, so long as it transgresses no Persian law.*

On the basis of this vignette, Karatani Kojin (2012/2017), somewhat like Hannah Arendt (1963) before but in much greater detail, construed the related term *isonomia* (ἰσονομία) as freedom from rule. Rather than freedom to self-rule, freedom from rule was linked by both Arendt and Karatani to equality before the law. Karatani elaborated on freedom from rule in terms of the political economy and political geography of Greek poleis in Classical Antiquity. The limited physical mobility, entrenchment of class relations including slavery, and exclusive citizenship in Athenian poleis led to migration to Ionian poleis where the supply of land was sufficiently abundant to allow more even distribution of resources and consequently, of wealth. Isonomia in this milieu was contingent upon the availability of unoccupied land capable of sustaining the livelihood of those fleeing intractable inequality. For Karatani, the primary mode of exchange in Athenian poleis was plunder and redistribution, and in Ionia, something more akin to reciprocity. Despite not being autocratic, or oligarchic, neither was Athenian democracy a realisation of the egalitarian ideals as envisioned by Herodotus' Otanes. Instead, among Athenian poleis a major discount was put on democracy through the exploitation of non-citizens and slaves.

From a world-historic perspective, isonomia is the result of replacing not only one environment for another, but also one set of exchange relations with another. Where isonomia does not prevail, equality is enjoyed by some at the expense of the freedom of others. Freedom is obtained by moving away from the locale of exclusion to one of non-exclusion. A locale of non-exclusion is one where resources could be accessed as needed rather than by reliance upon gifting, provisioning, or transacting. Although physical mobility is itself a kind of freedom, its own ability to effect isonomia is severely limited by the finite land resources by which state territory is normally defined. As an ideal then, isonomia provides a way of conceptualising equality in terms of exchange relations. Figure 3.1 offers a typology of equality by major modes of exchange.

Contingent as it is upon exchange relations, equality is neither hyperbolic nor complete. Subjugation is a fundamental feature in all modes of exchange except under isonomia, or Mode "D". Under mode "A", inequality in resource access could be resolved by means of gift exchange. Under mode "B", rulers assume the mantle of protector and provide for the majority in return for their subservience. Under mode "C", nominal equality exists in market transactions where commodities including labour are exchanged through the medium of money. Finally, under conditions where rule becomes irrelevant or unnecessary, social, economic, and political distinctions fade into insignificance.

B: equality in need	A: equality in belonging
plunder and redistribution	*reciprocity*
C: equality in opportunity in principle	D: equality through freedom from rule
commodity exchange	*isonomia*

Fig. 3.1 Inequality under major modes of exchange. Compare with those in Karatani (2008, 2010/2014, 2012/2017)

The four major modes of exchange merely make up a schematic of the kinds of inequality perpetuated in different social formations from a world-historic perspective. For the context in question, not only is inequality manifest as differential entitlements to public goods and services among urban residents, it is also evident in the uneven distribution of resources required for these entitlements to be realised. Notable among these are educational resources found in public schools and disparities between these schools. Hence even for non-householder urban residents to whom public education services are offered through changes to local policy, there would still be many other barriers in the way of equality in education (see especially Liu et al., 2017). State attempts at equalisation of public service entitlements are particularly significant in light of the array of policy and non-policy barriers. To the extent that inequality is intractable and that the state presents itself as mitigating inequality, it would be pertinent to ask which "logics of social stratification" (Esping-Andersen, 1990, p. 77) could be identified in policies of the Chinese state, irrespective of where China fits within any typology of welfare-state regimes. The appearance of any such logics would entail not just the symbolic construction of equality and freedom from inequality, but also of policy measures which promote these qualities in administration, not to mention the grounds on which these measures, and resulting fractions, are justified.

3.2.4 Relations Between State and Societal Agents

In the context in question, internal migrants find themselves in exchange relations in different parts of state territory, with different branches of the state, with each other, and with established local householders. The most relevant unit of analysis here is that of the collective of residents on the one hand, and of state institutions on the other. Their agency in public service entitlement equalisation is conceived not as individual but as collective.

Among state institutions, agentive relations have already been identified of mutual dependence in the generation of fiscal income and fulfilment of fiscal responsibility (e.g. Wang & Rong, 2019). Agentive relations are typically structured by lines of responsibility which traverse administrative divisions as well as the functional divisions into bureaus within each. Further, it should be noted that trans-agentive relations are also implicated. Trans-agentive relations may be manifest for instance where the central government somehow shares the agency of local authorities, for instance by assuming it, and vice versa. Accordingly, state institutions are not necessarily assumed to share the same logic behind the mitigation of inequality through policy (cf. Esping-Andersen, 1990).

In turn, non-householder urban residents have the opportunity to respond to the policy initiatives of government administration. In respect of public goods and services in urban districts, these residents could for example engage in competition with each other for a chance to become new citizens, thereby earning the full set of entitlements in the process (see Sect. 2.5). Without additional resources, more established householders share a limited amount of locally provided public goods and services with new citizens, with further demand coming from those residents who remain resident but lack local household registration. The exchanges between the central government, local authorities, non-householder residents and householder residents are represented schematically in Table 3.1. Each collective implicated in exchange relations can be further sub-divided.

Table 3.1 Schematic representation of the combinations of parties involved in forming exchange relations in the equalisation of public service entitlements in any given city in China

Exchange relations in entitlement equalisation		
Central Government, Institution 1	↔	Local Government 1, Institution 1
Local Government 1, Institution 1	↔	Local Government 1, Institution 2
Central Government, Institution 1	↔	Non-householder Residents
Local Government 1, Institution 1	↔	Non-householder Residents
Local Government 1, Institution 2	↔	Non-householder Residents
Local Government 2, Institution 1	↔	Non-householder Residents
Local Government 2, Institution 2	↔	Non-householder Residents
Central Government, Institution 1	↔	Established Local Residents
Local Government 1, Institution 1	↔	Established Local Residents
Local Government 1, Institution 2	↔	Established Local Residents
Local Government 2, Institution 1	↔	Established Local Residents
Local Government 2, Institution 2	↔	Established Local Residents
Non-householder Residents	↔	Non-householder Residents
Non-householder Residents	↔	Established Local Residents
Established Local Residents	↔	Established Local Residents

With a relatively fuller specification of the parties to exchange and their potential relations with each other, inequality in a particular respect, for instance public education, can be more clearly seen as an issue not only for non-householder residents, but for established local residents also. Irrespective of policy settings, urban residents of different designations can be expected to exert pressures on limited educational resources. Hence for state institutions, equalisation of entitlements to public school entry would be a matter of responding in various ways to the demands of two major collectives of societal agents, namely, local householders as well as migrants. In the process, state institutions also need to respond to each other's demands in respect of this policy domain, not to mention those in respect of other domains.

3.3 Public Service Provision as Multi-party Exchange

3.3.1 Urban Scale and Administrative Rank

In the parlance of the 2014 national framework regulating permanent settlement of internal migrants, Suzhou is an ultra-large city (see Sect. 2.5.2). As discussed in the previous chapter, the urban scale on which Suzhou is ranked in this way is based on the size of the ordinarily resident population in the urban core. As such, this urban scale is imbued with two kinds of stratification logic, both of which are realised by means of symbolic differentiation. First, the urban is divided dichotomously, typically into areas surrounding the seat of the prefectural government as opposed to those of adjacent counties. Secondly, ranked by population in the urban core, cities become symbolically divided between those with less presumed capacity versus those with more presumed capacity to absorb migrants. Thus intertwined, a justification exists for more populous cities to issue relatively restrictive settlement and service provision policies.

The urban core, however, like other territorial categories, is subject to symbolic construction. In 2012, the urban core of Suzhou almost doubled in area by the incorporation of Wujiang, an augmentation of 1092.9 km^2 (see Fig. 3.2). This also meant a considerable increase to the population within the urban core, or 31.1% based on figures as of the end of 2011. Without such a major change in administrative division in 2012, which was duly approved by the central government, it

Fig. 3.2 Administrative divisions within the Municipality of Suzhou, Jiangsu Province (*Source* https://www.suzhou.gov.cn/szsenglish/szxzqh/202106/78b 84cd38dfb4fb1b60ed21cc60336c6.shtml)

would not have been possible for Suzhou to lay claim to ultra-large city status in the policy milieu exemplified by the 2014 national regulatory framework (see Sect. 2.5.2). As of the end of 2015, the ordinarily resident population of the urban core of Suzhou rose to 5.5 million, with Wujiang contributing 1.3 million. In exchange for lifting the prefectural city's ranking on the urban scale, Wujiang was reportedly allowed to preserve a degree of administrative autonomy for five years, that is, until the end of 2017 (Cartier, 2016). Hence despite losing its status as a county-level city, the district of Wujiang was able to continue exercising its former prerogatives in policy-making. Analyses conducted as part of the present study revealed that Wujiang continued to make its own policies up to the end of 2020, well beyond the transition period apparently agreed to before administrative boundaries were redrawn back in 2012. As central government calls for district administrators within ultra-large cities to devise their own citizenisation points-systems were not publicly issued until after 2017 (e.g. National Development and Reform Commission, 2018), Wujiang's agency in policy-making since 2012 could not be taken superficially as a response to directives from the top. Remarkably then, as a result of exchanges between levels of administration, Suzhou and Wujiang have in recent years been operating parallel citizenisation programmes, and as shall be presented below, programmes in conferring upon non-householder residents access to publicly provided educational and medical services.

As already noted by researchers, changes to administrative division are also changes to lines of reporting and lines of fiscal credit (e.g. Ma, 2005). The redivision of Suzhou in 2012 was however not simply an isolated exercise in restructuring the administrative hierarchy within which local governance could be carried out (Cartier, 2016). Nation-wide, there had been prior policy attempts to address the fiscal burden on local authorities in the provision of public services. These attempts culminated in high-level calls (e.g. National People's Congress, 2011) to reconfigure the relationship between prefectural-level cities and counties that cities had been empowered to lead since the late 1970s. Into this milieu entered provincial authorities that were meaning to take over from prefectural authorities the financing of public services offered within counties and county-level cities. This rebalancing of exchange relations across levels of administration, known as "province managing county finances directly",[2] has been regarded by some commentators as a way of reducing the kind of intra-urban disparity in public service provision resulting from the urban core retaining a disproportionately larger share of fiscal resources (e.g. Zhou, 2014). Against this broader policy background, the incorporation of Wujiang into Suzhou's urban core in 2012 could be interpreted as a strategy of consolidating control over both fiscal income and expenditure at the prefectural level. Significantly, it was in the same year that Kunshan, another county-level city under Suzhou, by far the strongest economic performer of four candidates, had had direct fiscal administration established over it by the Province of Jiangsu (Cartier, 2016). These developments within the jurisdiction of Suzhou underscore the unequal political-economic basis on which ranked state entities enter into exchange with each other and the potential implications these may have for residents under their administration. With the possible interdependence of political opportunity structure and social opportunity structure in mind then, exchanges between state and societal actors for public service entitlements may be pre-determined to an extent by exchanges between state actors for the requisite fiscal resources. As shall be seen below, the Province of Jiangsu was to maintain the above pattern of inter-agentive presence in respect of public service provision within the prefectural boundaries of Suzhou in the years leading up to 2021.

3.3.2   *Equalisation as an Evolving Policy Agenda*

The rhetoric of equalising public service provision for internal migrants resident in cities did not originate in the policy period in question. As early as in 2002, *The Scientific Outlook on Development* (or The Outlook in short, see Sect. 2.4.1) envisioned full coverage of the ordinarily resident urban population for basic public services. A less aspirational view was found in the 11th Five-year Plan (National People's Congress, 2006), where for instance full coverage of the urban population was referred to as a principle (Chapter 19) and a direction (Chapter 47) rather than a target. An early mention was made there of direct fiscal administration of counties by provinces in support of equalisation, but only for those localities with the necessary capacity (Chapter 32). Even then, equalisation

---

[2] That is, 省直管县财政 (shěng zhíguǎn xiàn cáizhèng).

was to be "progressed gradually", that is, phased in over time. An injunction against the redirection of funds reserved for public service provision into other public uses (Chapter 20) was especially suggestive of agentive relations among state entities over fiscal matters.

The rhetoric did however intensify in policy documents within the 12th Five-year Plan (2011–2015) period and 13th Five-year Plan (2016–2020) periods. While the same teleological gradualism as in *The Outlook* was discernible, principles of resource allocation towards the goal of equalisation were operationalised, probably for the first time, in the 12th Five-year Plan itself (National People's Congress, 2011). In Chapter 47, which was concerned with the deepening of fiscal-institutional reform, increased flexibility in inter-governmental transfers was stipulated by means including the rationalisation of special purpose funds. The latitude of not employing available funds for public service provision was thereby more formally reduced for local authorities than before 2011. The scope of coverage took a rhetorical turn by including rural as well as urban areas, making the 12th Five-year Plan even more ambitious than *The Outlook* in this particular respect, although the latter, unlike the former, referred to population coverage, not territorial coverage. This subtle but important change in emphasis was perhaps more consistent with the promise of equality for all irrespective of their place of residence, one that would nonetheless have to be delivered progressively rather than immediately. Gradually widening population coverage was also specified as a developmental principle in *The System of Basic Public Services—Companion to The Twelfth Five-year Plan* (State Council, 2012). This companion to the 12th Five-year Plan also required authorities in economically prosperous areas such as the Yangtze River Delta and Pearl River Delta to take the lead in unifying the rural and urban systems of public service provision. Central government calls for equalisation were duly echoed by provincial authorities such as those in Jiangsu (Province of Jiangsu, 2013), which administers 13 prefecture-level cities including Suzhou. Towards the end of the 12th Five-year Plan period, the reversal of institutionalised bifurcation, both rural–urban and urban-urban, through equalisation, was envisioned in *The National New-type Urbanisation Plan (2014–2020)* (Central Committee of the Communist Party of China & State Council, 2014).

The sense of urgency was even more evident by the time of the release of the 13th Five-year Plan (National People's Congress, 2016), according to which the extent of both citizenisation and equalisation were to be increased, along with an enhanced system of incentivising local authorities to integrate non-householder residents (Chapter 32). Eastern China, where Jiangsu and Suzhou are located, was tasked with increased economic co-operation and competitiveness in the international arena, a regional responsibility to be fulfilled through a high degree of equalisation (Chapter 37). In contrast, the western region was required to speed up the progress of equalisation in order to achieve economic growth through population growth. Scope of coverage was to be an issue once again in *Notice Regarding the Progress of Basic Public Services Equalisation—Companion to The Thirteenth Five-year Plan* (State Council, 2017), whereby full coverage of the population ordinarily resident in urban areas, the formulation in *The Outlook*, was reinstated, and contrasted with other, especially rural, settings in which equalisation was to be realised by other policy means. The ever-widening scope of equalisation required by this companion to the 13th Five-year Plan stood in sharp contrast with the limited scope of citizenisation. Significantly, the companion also defined equalisation as equal opportunity in access to public services as opposed to the literally equal distribution of these services.

The abovementioned central and provincial instruments of authority spawned an array of follow-up policies, especially at the municipal level of administration, from 2015 onwards. As already noted above, in parallel with the Municipality of Suzhou, the District of Wujiang had also been issuing its own policies within the period in question. Under this exceptional arrangement, instruments of authority issued by Suzhou were applicable to all parts of its urban core except Wujiang (Municipality of Suzhou, 2015a, 2015b). Conversely, policies issued by Wujiang were only applicable within the district but not elsewhere in Suzhou's urban core (District of Wujiang, 2014a, 2014b, 2016a, 2016b). In both jurisdictions defined under this arrangement, equalisation of access to publicly funded services was provided for by regulations governing citizenisation points-systems, whose form was examined in the previous chapter (see Sect. 2.5.3). Accordingly, applicants could seek to be made new citizens, and thereby being granted comprehensive entitlements to public services, or the less substantial alternative of a limited subset of public services in the educational or medical category. Eligible applicants could in fact enter their bids for all three programmes simultaneously in any given round. With the programmes arranged in this form, applicants were to compete with each other for the extent to which they met the same set of selection criteria specified in local policy. The programmes differed in respect of thresholds which applicants needed to exceed with the total number of points accumulated on the basis of selection criteria. Local authorities left room for themselves to set thresholds according to the amount of resources available to serve successful applicants-to-be. With the forms taken by points-systems in mind then, thresholds were in effect minimum socio-demographic and socio-economic offers applicants needed to make to a local authority in exchange for a successful bid. Remarkably, central government provisions for points-systems were intended only for the selective admission of new citizens, and not the selective conferring of public service entitlements upon non-householder residents (see State Council, 2012, 2017).

The conflation of equalisation with citizenisation in the policies of Suzhou and Wujiang was not a province-wide or nation-wide practice (cf. Wan & Vickers, 2021). Such conflation was inconsistent with the rhetoric produced by the central government and provincial authorities in a number of ways. First, by employing merit-based selection in determining public service entitlements, such services became less public by definition. Secondly, by widening the concept of new citizens to include those with lesser access to basic public services than others in the same urban locale, the very notion of equal opportunity embedded in the terms equalisation was compromised. Thirdly, the co-existence of parallel programmes in the urban core and one of its districts, neither of which was by itself ultra large in 2015, contradicted the principle of greater migrant absorption by less populous cities that was meant to be reinforced in the 2014 version of the urban scale. A different policy agenda was therefore discernible at the municipal and sub-municipal levels.

3.3.3   Recursion of Policy Form and Function

Equalisation policies in Suzhou and Wujiang appeared not to have reproduced those of the Province of Jiangsu or the central government. As already shown in terms of the inverted barrier of residential property purchase in Suzhou's points-system (Sect. 2.5.3), any superficial convergence with central policy form did not necessarily mean convergence with central policy function. In contrast, closer correspondence both in form and function was generally found between policies issued by Suzhou and Wujiang, whereby for instance a minimum amount of floor-space was specified for local residential property purchase that would result in the awarding of points. The minimum for Suzhou and Wujiang was

75 m^2 and 60 m^2 respectively. In both jurisdictions, additional residential properties meeting the floor-space criterion attracted additional points. Inverted barriers like property purchase and age were to eventually draw explicit criticism from provincial authorities, which characterised them as "hidden barriers" to be demolished (Province of Jiangsu, 2019). The rebuke was explicitly directed at Nanjing and Suzhou, the only two cities in the province whose urban core areas were sufficiently populous to be deemed ultra large and therefore eligible to operate point-systems. Suzhou was instructed to studiously follow national provisions for ultra-large cities uniformly within its entire jurisdiction to effect the orderly distribution and movement of the population. In the following year, and with only a few months before the end of the policy period in question, the Municipality of Suzhou released revisions to its points-system (Municipality of Suzhou, 2020a, 2020b). In the revised version, the inverted barrier of age was duly removed but not that of property purchase. The degree of inequity associated with the barrier was somewhat reduced by allowing only one purchased property 75 m^2 or larger to be counted and capping the number of points awarded at 100, down from 200 in the original version. In respect of the provincial requirement for policy uniformity, Wujiang was brought back into the governance fold of the urban core of Suzhou, effectively ending the independent, district-level points-system after it had been in operation for six years. It was not until the end of 2021 however that district authorities sought to rescind the relevant policies (namely, District of Wujiang, 2016a, 2016b). In examining the recursion of citizenisation and equalisation policies, therefore, the unfolding of inter-agentive exchange relations among central, provincial, municipal and district players came clearly into view. Under the auspices of central government policies, provincial authorities had had district-level policy-making, one of the sources of intra-urban disparity, removed from Suzhou's policy landscape.

3.4   EQUALISATION OF ACCESS TO PUBLIC EDUCATION

The rather extraordinary intervention of provincial authorities in Suzhou did not have the effect of entirely ending policy inducement of intra-urban disparity. Most pre-2021 policy levers, whether or not authorised at higher levels, remained at the disposal of the municipality. One such lever was the differential in citizenisation threshold set for the urban core and county-level cities. Ironically, as a result of policy changes, applicants hoping to settle in Wujiang since 2021 would have to score even more highly than in previous years. Even for those simply wishing to reside in Wujiang while enjoying limited public services, it became necessary to compete with those able to afford to purchase larger and more expensive residential properties elsewhere in the urban core.

In respect of the equalisation of access to publicly funded education, the points-system continued to act as a way for the municipality to operate highly localised public educational services. Even before citizenisation and equalisation were made into priorities in 2014, local policy-makers already had to contend with disparities among public schools under their jurisdiction (see Liu et al., 2017 for a case study of an unnamed city in the province). Some of these disparities were the combined result of institutional arrangements across policy domains such as changes to administrative divisions, city administration of counties, direct fiscal administration by the province in the case of Kunshan, county-level administration of education in the first grade to the ninth grade, and student catchment areas set up accordingly at the sub-county, that is, district level. The emphasis upon equalisation, especially in the latter years of the decade in question, was not the removal of all extant supply-side disparities in public education, but rather the barriers which prevented non-householders from even competing with householders in sending their children to local public schools (see especially State Council, 2017). In Suzhou, the opportunity to compete for school entry was duly provided, albeit in the form of the points-system, and with lower thresholds than those seeking to be made local householders. Apparently due to variations in supply, a different threshold was set for each school in each annual round of application, along with an admission quota for the children of non-householders. Each child of each applicant was restricted to nominating one school whose catchment area enveloped the local place of residence. Applicants over the school-level threshold were then ranked according to accumulated points and notified if they were within the school-level quota. Applicants excluded by quotas were subsequently notified to see if they were willing to accept places offered to their children by the district-level education bureau, again on the basis of ranking by accumulated points. Under local policy in Suzhou then, school entry for non-native children required the confluence of a large number of institutional, household, and applicant factors. The number of places initially made available for the year 2020 under the influence of these factors are listed against the number of participating schools in Table 3.2.

Table 3.2 The number of places available to the children of non-householder residents and the number of schools participating in the relevant equalisation programme in Suzhou in the year 2020

Level of education	Places	Participating schools	Average places per participating school
Primary school			
• Suzhou—Urban Core	8201	100	82
• Suzhou—Wujiang District	2295	56	41
Junior high school			
• Suzhou—Urban Core	5251	73	72
• Suzhou—Wujiang District	1584	29	55

As shown in Table 3.2, the number of places available in each participating school varied. These variations were indicative of the unevenness of multi-party exchanges in the local political economy and local political geography. For their part, municipal and district authorities contributed to this unevenness by managing school participation in the equalisation effort. Taking the total number of educational institutions in 2019 as the base, only 44.5% and 46.1% of available primary and junior secondary schools were allowed to serve the children of applicants in the urban core in 2020. In Wujiang, the rate of participation by primary schools was at 100% due to the involvement of private institutions of education with support of the district bureau of education. This recent move by Wujiang authorities, which actually echoed central government calls to effect public–private partnerships in public service provision (National People's Congress, 2016; State Council, 2012), highlighted commercial entities as yet another party to exchange in equalisation.

Apart from private schools, property developers had proven to be crucial in the operation of the district-level education market. Prices in urban district-level housing markets were shown to respond sensitively to the presence or absence of schools with strong academic records (cf. Wen et al., 2017; Xu et al., 2018). The mutual stimulation of the two markets was further catalysed by the planned participation of reputable schools in equalisation. Despite being free in principle then, public education had by virtue of multi-party exchanges become a public good consumed on the condition of indirect costs borne by urban residents. For householder residents and non-household residents, indirect costs would be incurred in the rental or purchase of property in reputable catchment areas. In turn, children may have to bear other indirect costs as they sought to achieve results in larger classes with fewer teachers in renowned schools.

At least in the case of Suzhou, lines of privilege drawn upon the urban landscape as a result of policy-induced exchanges over public education overlapped in such complex ways that they had practically become woven into the social fabric of the city. Instead of manifesting as distinct social strata, schools of different levels of academic performance have, like the cities in which they are located, absorbed to different degrees residents with differing socio-demographic and socio-economic profiles. What equalisation of access to public education appeared to have created were the smallest possible fractions of land into which individual members of the nation could be accommodated: seats in the urban classroom. The mutual imbrication of territory and population in policy-making by higher levels of administration thereby found expression on a much more delicate scale in implementation by local authorities.

3.5   IDEALS, INEQUITIES, AND IMPERATIVES

3.5.1   *Freedom to Trade and Policy Sophistication*

Analysis in the current chapter has demonstrated the extension of selectivity in urban citizen-making to urban studentship under the rubric of equalisation in policy documents issued by levels of public administration in China since 2011. Selectivity is evident not only in the minutiae of which urban school places are made available to whose parents through state policy, and how many, but also in the precise urban locations of residence adopted by parents at large. In turn, the selectivity seen in the behaviour of these parties to exchange is also partly a result of discretion exercised by property developers with reference to catchment area boundaries set by local authorities. Unlike in earlier policy periods, the last decade saw the widespread introduction of state-run competitions, each somewhat different in form and function as provided for by the central government, through which the children of non-householder residents are admitted into schools across Chinese cities. In turn, this has intensified the larger competition for entry into preferred public schools throughout urban China.

By their very own selective offers, parties to exchange enable each other's needs to be met, however imperfectly, but only together with mutually imposed constraints. There is no evidence to suggest that any party to exchange seeks to avoid these constraints by setting aside their respective demands on each other, which include urbanisation by a select population on the part of the state, social mobility for the next generation on the part of urban residents, and an expansive real estate market on the part of property developers. Instead, governance, residency, education, and housing seem to reinforce each other precisely by having the ideal of distributive justice relinquished. While the latest policy provides freedom to all residents to trade locally with state and commercial entities over public education, trading rules are typically such that some residents will remain unable or unwilling to expend their resources just to enter a competition with no guarantee of outcome. The uncertainty and unfairness of such competitions have nonetheless not prevented other residents from taking part. Such participation is a sign of purposive rationality under the steering influence of state policy and its orchestration of capital flows (see Sect. 1.2.4). Despite tremendous variations in detail, educational entitlement equalisation policies are mostly an invitation issued by the state to internal migrants to calculate the worth of foregoing resources in return for securing the long-term future of their children through publicly funded education. Internal migrants are of course free to pursue alternative avenues and the trading opportunities therein: entry into the state-run competition of another city, private education in some urban setting or other, private or public education in the place of origin, and so forth.

As components of China's urbanisation policy, citizenisation, and equalisation illustrate rather clearly a continuing shift in the state's self-presentation towards ideals along the dimensions of coherence, progress, and sophistication (see Sects. 1.3.3 and 1.4.2). The state's role in effecting a whole-of-government response to the perennial issue of fiscal burden in public service provision is showcased for instance in the mobilisation of resources across multiple levels of administration and state institutions. Thus integrated, the entire nation's progress towards urbanisation, especially through its population, is said to support agricultural modernisation, industrialisation, and information technologisation. These advancements are however contingent upon the diverse utilisation of state capacity as manifest for example in policy attempts to selectively incentivise some segments of the population to migrate to certain urban destinations without settling, and others to settle there permanently, and still others, to remain there or return to the place of origin. As such, the dense, multi-layered differentiation of territory and population in service of state imperatives displays considerable policy sophistication. The ideological commitment to such diversity in statecraft has the important implication that inequality will recur, and take on new forms and functions along with the policies which sustain it. Intractable inequality resulting from policy sophistication is counter-balanced by the fraught freedom of choice between different modes of belonging to the nation, and by implication, different modes of exchange with the state. Although fraught with inequality, freedom from unrelenting socio-demographic comparison and socio-economic participation in urban life is perhaps a kind of isonomia. The fostering of multiple kinds of political kinship on a continuum marked by freedom *to* trade and freedom *from* trade is perhaps one of the most significant features of policy from the period in question. This finding is at odds with accounts of unitary state power employed to stratify society and privilege the few with no agenda other than regime survival (e.g. Zhang, 2018), migrant selection (e.g. Dong & Goodburn, 2020), or population control more generally (e.g. Wan & Vickers, 2021). The observable tendencies of diversification in policy suggest however that Chinese state may well have additional agendas, and stratification logics, that are arguably more sophisticated than the above.

3.5.2   *Freedom to Rule and Modes of Exchange*

The dominance of commodity exchange in relations between the state and urban residents in ultra-large cities and mega cities is particularly prominent in recent educational entitlement equalisation policies (see Fig. 3.1). In also considering the number and kind of official parties to exchange in these settings, however, it becomes clear that exchange *within* the state incompletely resembles exchange *with* the state in a number of paradigmatically germane ways. First, levels of public administration beneath the central government are themselves subject to cross-classification. For instance, the county has been symbolically constructed by policy as rural or urban, and further, as being administered by the municipality or even higher up by the province. Secondly, even such classifications are mutable, as for example in the making of a county into an urban district of the municipality and thus out of the scope of direct fiscal administration by the province. Thirdly, in policy documents levels of government like counties, municipalities, and provinces are themselves constructed as objects of administration between which disparities could be identified and for which differential measures would as a result need to be applied. As in exchanges with the state, exchanges within the state take place between parties of unequal standing on the basis of the instrumental foregoing of autonomy. What parties offer to each other in exchange through the medium of money is therefore more than simply commodities. In addition to fiscal transfers, local authorities could offer greater throughput of centrally issued policy, perhaps inversely to the extent their jurisdictions are depended upon to realise state imperatives such as economic growth and social stability. Official parties to exchange with greater leverage in this regard would be more likely to produce policies in a heterologous relationship with those from above (see Sect. 1.4.3). Those with less bargaining power could nonetheless find a degree of freedom in constructing policies in a hemilogous relationship with their municipal or provincial counterparts.

3.5.3   Redistribution Matters

Under the prevailing conditions of world capitalism, state policy in China serves as a major domestic platform on which symbolic differentiation, and its eventual impact upon valorisation and competition, can be managed. Irrespective of the combination of parties to exchange, and terms of exchange beyond commodities, the main principle of operation remains the conversion of symbolically constructed differences into capital gains. From this perspective, urbanisation is the policy-driven and highly strategic capitalisation of fractions of territory by means of the similarly strategic redistribution of fractions of population. Population fractions thereby guided to reside in cities are themselves capitalised to various degrees so that their collective consumptive capacity can be increased. By design then, this kind of urbanisation is meant to be sustained by entitlement equalisation rather than sustaining it *per se*. Instead of being fully precluded, however, state redistribution of resources in support of urban residents in the largest cities in the nation recedes far behind the policy landscape and into the praxis of government. Discernible nonetheless is the state's efforts in resource redistribution in support of population redistribution into these cities. As for all other members of the nation, who have apparently opted to live under other political-economic and political-geographic conditions, demands for public services are met through additional policies and other types of inter-governmental transfers under the auspices of other state projects.

REFERENCES

Arendt, H. (1963). *On revolution*. Penguin.

Cartier, C. (2016). A political economy of rank: The territorial administrative hierarchy and leadership mobility in urban China. *Journal of Contemporary China, 25*(100), 529–546. https://doi.org/10.1080/10670564.2015.113 2771

Cartier, C., & Hu, D. (2020). Suzhou and the city-region: The administrative divisions in historical perspective and rural-urban transition. In B. Tang & P. Cheung (Eds.), *Suzhou in transition: Social change and development in contemporary China* (pp. 193–213). Routledge.

Central Committee of the Communist Party of China, & State Council. (2014). *National new-type urbanisation plan (2014–2020)*. The People's Press.

Cheung, P. (2021). Location-specific citizenship: State visions of spatial selectivity in the cities of Beijing and Suzhou. *Territory, Politics, Governance*. https://doi.org/10.1080/21622671.2021.1982760

District of Wujiang. (2014a). *Details of implementation of the new citizenship points-system in Wujiang, Suzhou* (Wuzhengban 2014 Number 126). http://www.zgwj.gov.cn/upfile/template/contentpage/zgwj_zwgknew/nry.aspx?ID=36022

District of Wujiang. (2014b). *Means of managing the new citizenship points-system in Wujiang, Suzhou* (Wuzhengguizi 2014 Number 2).

District of Wujiang. (2016a). *Means of managing the new citizenship points-system in Wujiang, Suzhou* (Revised) (Wuzhengguizi 2016 Number 1). http://www.zgwj.gov.cn/images/52169152fce6ca3a69923667 b8a6f52e/20161110141224493123.doc

District of Wujiang. (2016b). *Scoring criteria for the new citizenship points-system in Wujiang, Suzhou* (Revised) (Wuzhengban 2016 Number 7). http://www.zgwj.gov.cn/images/ea1700d90abe996ab582a946 0491f98a/20161110141422026961.doc

Dong, Y. M., & Goodburn, C. (2020). Residence permits and points systems: New forms of educational and social stratification in Urban China. *Journal of Contemporary China, 29*(125), 647–666. https://doi.org/10.1080/106 70564.2019.1704997

Esping-Andersen, G. (1990). *The three worlds of welfare capitalism*. Polity Press.

Goodman, D. S. G. (2014). *Class in contemporary China*. Wiley.

Herodotus. (1921). *Herodotus, with an English translation by A.D. Godley* (A. D. Godley, Trans., Vol. II). Heinemann.

Herodotus. (1998). *Herodotus: The histories* (R. Waterfield, Trans.). Oxford University Press.

Herodotus. (2005). *The histories* (G. C. Macaulay & D. Lateiner, Trans.). Barnes & Noble Classics.

Hobbes, T. (1675). *The history of the Grecian War in Eight Books*. London: Charles Harper.

Karatani, K. (2008). Beyond capital-nation-state. *Rethinking Marxism, 20*(4), 569–595. https://doi.org/10.1080/08935690802299447

Karatani, K. (2010/2014). *The structure of world history* (M. K. Bourdaghs, Trans.). Duke University Press.

Karatani, K. (2012/2017). *Isonomia and the origins of philosophy* (J. A. Murphy, Trans.). Duke University Press.

Liu, S., Sun, W., & Barrow, E. (2017). Promises and practices: A case study on compulsory education policy implementation in a large migrant-inflow city in China. *Second international handbook of urban education* (pp. 133–149). Springer International Publishing.

Ma, L. J. C. (2005). Urban administrative restructuring, changing scale relations and local economic development in China. *Political Geography, 24*(4), 477–497.

Municipality of Suzhou. (2015a). *Means of managing the points-system for the transient population* (Sufuguizi 2015 Number 6). http://www.zfxxgk.suz hou.gov.cn/sxqzf/szsrmzf/201512/t20151214_654708.html

Municipality of Suzhou. (2015b). Scoring criteria of the points-system for the transient population (Sufuguizi 2015 Number 7). http://www.zfxxgk.suz hou.gov.cn/sjjg/szszffzbgs/201601/t20160118_668648.html

Municipality of Suzhou. (2020a). Means of managing the points-system for the transient population (Sufuguizi 2020 Number 15). https://www.suzhou.gov. cn/szsrmzf/zfwj/202011/53f6b237c13f4bf1b09df5accd14053d.shtml

Municipality of Suzhou. (2020b). Scoring criteria of the points-system for the transient population (Sufuguizi 2020 Number 16). https://www.suzhou.gov. cn/szsrmzf/zfwj/202011/5f567825d58d48ed8e3353f971bff6c5.shtml

National Development and Reform Commission. (2018). *Notice concerning key tasks in the implementation of new-type urbanization in 2018*. http://www. gov.cn/xinwen/2018-03/13/content_5273637.htm

National People's Congress. (2006). *Outline of the eleventh five-year plan of the economy and society of the People's Republic of China*. http://www.gov.cn/gon gbao/content/2006/content_268766.htm

National People's Congress. (2011). *Outline of the twelfth five-year plan of the economy and society of the People's Republic of China*. http://www.gov.cn/201 1lh/content_1825838.htm

National People's Congress. (2016). *Outline of the thirteenth five-year plan of the economy and society of the People's Republic of China*. http://paper.peo ple.com.cn/rmrb/html/2016-03/18/nw.D110000renmrb_20160318_1-01. htm

Province of Jiangsu. (2013). *Notice concerning the issuing of the means of managing the residency of the transient population* (Suzhengbanfa (2013) Number 179). http://www.jiangsu.gov.cn/jsgov/tj/bgt/201311/W02013 1119521174530115.doc

Province of Jiangsu. (2019). Opinion on the promotion of permanent settlement of the non-registered population (Suzhengbanfa 2019 Number 90). http://www.js.gov.cn/art/2020/1/7/art_64797_8903162.html

Saich, T. (2008). *Providing public goods in transitional China*. Palgrave Macmillan.

Shang Yang. (1928). *The book of Lord Shang* (J. J. Duyvendak, Trans.). Probsthain.

Solinger, D. J. (1993). China's transients and the state: A form of civil society? *Politics and Society, 21*(1), 91–122.

Solinger, D. J. (1999). *Contesting citizenship in urban China*. University of California Press.

Solinger, D. J. (2006). The creation of a new underclass in China and its implications. *Environment and Urbanization, 18*(1), 177.

State Council. (2012). *Notice regarding the issuing of the system of basic public services—Companion to the twelfth five-year plan* (Guofa (2012) Number 29). http://www.gov.cn/zwgk/2012-07/20/content_2187242.htm

State Council. (2017). *Notice regarding the progress of basic public services equalisation—Companion to the thirteenth five-year plan* (Guofa (2017) Number 9). http://www.gov.cn/zhengce/content/2017-03/01/content_5172013.htm

Wan, Y., & Vickers, E. (2021). Towards meritocratic apartheid? Points systems and migrant access to China's Urban Public Schools. *China Quarterly.* https://doi.org/10.1017/s0305741021000990

Wang, X. (2020). Permits, points, and permanent household registration: Recalibrating Hukou Policy under "top-level design." *Journal of Current Chinese Affairs, 49*(3), 269–290. https://doi.org/10.1177/1868102619894739

Wang, X., & Rong, X. (2019). Variations in educational inequalities in China and policy implications. In J. Yu & S. Guo (Eds.), *The Palgrave handbook of local governance in contemporary China* (pp. 509–540). Palgrave Macmillan.

Wen, H. Z., Xiao, Y., & Zhang, L. (2017). School district, education quality, and housing price: Evidence from a natural experiment in Hangzhou, China. *Cities, 66*, 72–80. https://doi.org/10.1016/j.cities.2017.03.008

Xu, Y., Song, W. X., & Liu, C. H. (2018). Social-spatial accessibility to urban educational resources under the school district system: A case study of public primary schools in Nanjing, China. *Sustainability, 10*(7). https://doi.org/10.3390/su10072305

Zhang, C. (2018). Governing neoliberal authoritarian citizenship: Theorizing hukou and the changing mobility regime in China. *Citizenship Studies, 22*(8), 855–881. https://doi.org/10.1080/13621025.2018.1531824

Zhou, T. (2014). The institutional shift from "city-leading-counties" to "province-leading counties". *Chinese Cadres Tribune* (07), 7–11. https://doi.org/10.14117/j.cnki.cn11-3331/d.2014.07.016

Zhou, X. (2004). *The state and the life chances in Urban China*. Cambridge University Press.

CHAPTER 4

Common Tongue and Urban Membership

Abstract Most members of the Chinese nation speak one of the many dialects comprising the Han language. Somewhat surprisingly, not every member of the Han ethnic majority speaks Mandarin, otherwise known as Putonghua. Against the background of region-specific policies aimed at urbanising China through internal migration, this chapter takes the relative obscurity of Chinese dialects in state policy as the starting point in an investigation of the state's position on nativism. The chapter asks what if anything the state wants to promote about the notion that life could not be given full expression outside the native place. In order to do so, the relationship between land and language is first overviewed briefly in terms of dialect geography, and separately of Chinese linguistic histo-riography. Linkages between land and language are then identified in a synoptic reading of language planning policy and population management policy. Analyses suggest that the state has been strategically ambivalent about residential nativism but not linguistic nativism.

Keywords Chinese dialects · Language planning · Mandarin · Nativism · Regional development

P. Cheung, *Statecraft in Symbols*,
https://doi.org/10.1007/978-981-19-3319-6_4

More than 100 million people from our rural areas are gradually becoming permanent residents in our cities. 13 million have found jobs, and construction has begun on 5.8 million new homes for those people living in dilapidated houses. Many have already moved into their new warm homes. Many people from Hong Kong, Macao, and Taiwan now have resident permits for the mainland, and Hong Kong has become a stop on our high-speed railway network. China, as a country of people on the move, is energetically pursuing prosperity. We are running at full speed towards the realization of our dreams.[1]

The man who finds his homeland sweet is still a tender beginner; he to whom every soil is as his native one is already strong; but he is perfect to whom the entire world is as a foreign land. The tender soul has fixed his love on one spot in the world; the strong man has extended his love to all places; the perfect man has extinguished his.[2]

4.1   ORIENTATION

In his nationwide address marking the end of 2018, Xi Jinping described the people of China as being energetically on the move. This was clearly a figure of speech which encapsulated physical mobility in the form of rural-to-urban migration as well as the social mobility migration implied. In their respective circumstances, members of the nation were said to be in full pursuit of their own dreams. Indeed, the statistics cited by Xi alluded to disparities within the national community and the efforts made by the state in response. The efforts were those aimed at solving what Premier Li Keqiang summed up earlier as "the three one-hundred million people problems" (Xinhua News Agency, 2014), namely, urbanisation of China by making 100 million people into permanent residents of cities to which they have migrated, construction of dwellings for another 100 million migrants living in shantytowns and urban villages, and finally, development of the central-west region to allow yet another 100 million

---

[1] Excerpted from http://chinaplus.cri.cn/news/politics/11/20181231/230041.html. The original reads "1亿多非户籍人口在城市落户的行动正在继续, 1300 万人在城镇找到了工作, 解决棚户区问题的住房开工了 580 万套, 新市民有了温暖的家。很多港澳台居民拿到了居住证, 香港进入了全国高铁网。一个流动的中国, 充满了繁荣发展的活力。我们都在努力奔跑, 我们都是追梦人" and can be found at http://www.qstheory.cn/yaowen/2018-12/31/c_1123931816.htm.

[2] Excerpted from p. 101 of Hugh of St Victor. (1120/1961). *The Didasalicon* (J. Taylor, Trans.). New York: Columbia University Press.

to take up employment in areas near their places of origin, all by 2020. The success of all these large-scale state projects would have depended on massive internal migration across varying physical, socio-demographic, and socio-economic distances, and in multiple directions within China. Bound up with the geographical, economic, and social challenges facing internal migrants are the much less salient, but no less significant ones of culture and language. Due to their diversity within Chinese territory, culture and language are themselves challenges in policy-induced internal migration. The state, for its part, has had a role in designing policy to manage the multi-cultural, multi-ethnic, and multilingual makeup of the Chinese nation. No matter how the Chinese language is defined, not every Chinese national speaks Chinese. In the absence of a common tongue, contact between members of the same nation could pose a serious problem for the kind of urbanisation that is based on internal migration. Even with a common tongue, absence from abode could itself create additional challenges in the regulation of mass population movements.

Against the above milieu, the current chapter examines state policy responses to disparities commonly called "social" and diversity loosely labelled "linguistic". These policies are drawn from domains including but not limited to those already examined in previous chapters. Of particular interest in this chapter is the symbolic construction of native land and native language, and how such constructions have varied in policies issued since the founding of the state in 1949. In order to allow these policies to be seen in context, the next section situates conceptual connections between land and language in China from the point of the collapse of the monarchy in 1911 onward, and does so with regards to the Han-speaking majority. This will be followed by a selective survey of previous work and an outline of specific aspects of symbolic construction of land and language in question. Reflections are offered after the synoptic reading of policy documents issued by the central government, provincial authorities of Jiangsu, and municipal authorities of Suzhou up to the end of 2020. The reading will be focussed on what particular constructions of land and language indicate of policy's position within the ideological matrix (see Sects. 1.3.3 and 1.4.2).

4.2   LAND AND LANGUAGE IN CHINA

4.2.1   Han Dialect Geography

In the twentieth century, many efforts were made to exemplify the details of the land–language relationship in China. Emblematic of these attempts were *The Language Atlas of China* (Baumann et al., 1988; Xiong et al., 2012) and *The Great Dictionary of Modern Chinese Dialects* (Li, 1999/2002). The first volume of *The Atlas* and all six books of *The Great Dictionary* are companions of each other in the sense of their focus upon the dialects of Hanyu (汉语, hànyǔ), the language of the Han ethnic majority. In these sources, dialects were shown to be *geolects* which exist in various possible kinds of taxonomic relationship with each other. In the absence of any definitive taxonomy, four to twelve dialect groups have been identified in different schemes of classification, with each scheme offering its own lists of sub-dialectal varieties and geographical referents (see Kurpaska, 2010). Another list of varieties is reflected in distribution maps in *The Atlas*, where territory is also given a taxonomic treatment. Specifically, dialect "locality" (点, diǎn) is nested within so-called "clusters" (小片, xiǎopiān), and in turn within "sub-groups" (片, piān), and "groups" (区, qū). Crucially, these geographical categories in *The Atlas* do not correspond directly to administrative divisions in China. In respect of the distribution of Wu (吴, wú) dialects, for example, clusters manifest themselves as sub-provincial and cross-provincial areas. Wu dialects are most commonly associated with the southern portion of Jiangsu province where Suzhou is located, the Municipality of Shanghai, and most of Zhejiang province. Dialects common in Jiangxi are also classified within the Wu group but found in less prominent sub-groups and clusters. Wu dialects can also be found spoken in smaller portions of Anhui and Fujian provinces.

As a whole, stable land–language relationships form the conceptual basis in works exemplified by *The Atlas* and *The Great Dictionary*. The stability of land–language relationships has however been considerably affected by the redrawing of administrative boundaries separating rural China from urban China and migration between the two since the early 1980s. In effect, the distribution of Hanyu dialects as described in *The Atlas* and *The Great Dictionary* does not account for the location of the residentially mobile proportion of the total population, estimated at between 8.3 and 26.6% in 2020 (see Sect. 2.5.1). Furthermore, urbanisa-tion-by-migration since the mid-1980s also problematises the conceptual distinctions separating geolects from other kinds of dialect.

Whether or not defined geographically, a key feature of Han dialects is mutual unintelligibility to its speakers. Technical difficulties in taxonomy aside, a pertinent distinction to be made with regards to mutual intelligibility is between Mandarin dialects and non-Mandarin dialects. According to *The Atlas*, there are three main vectors in the distribution of Mandarin and non-Mandarin dialects. Historically, non-Mandarin dialects are distributed along coastal areas of the southeast in a generally north-easterly direction (see Fig. 4.1). Again historically, Mandarin dialects are distributed along two axes, one also in a generally north-easterly direction, but much further inland from the East China Sea. Another vector along

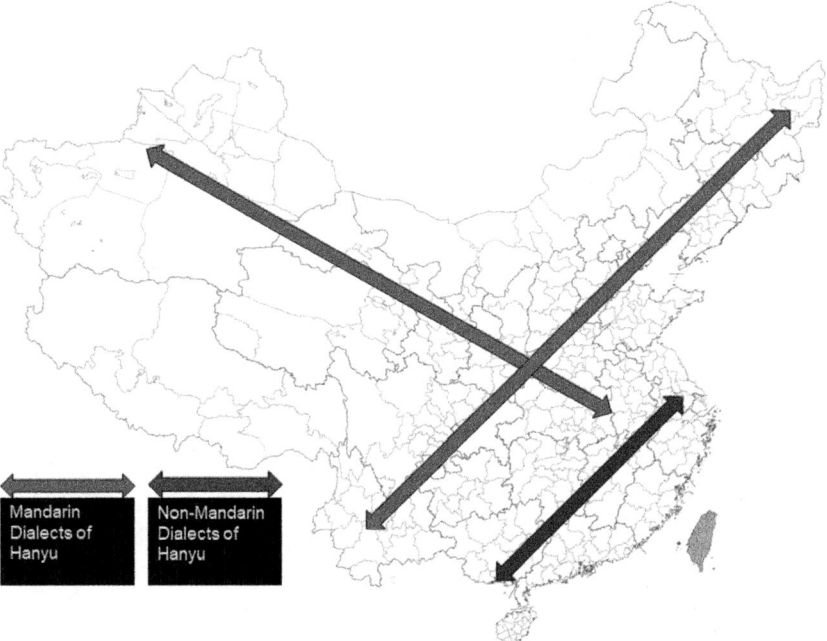

Fig. 4.1 Han dialect distribution vectors (Adapted from https://commons.wik imedia.org/wiki/File:Blank_map_of_China_with_prefecture-level_divisions.png)

which Mandarin dialects are distributed stretches out in a generally north-westerly direction, and almost perpendicularly to the north-easterly one. A higher degree of linguistic similarity can generally be found between any given pair of Mandarin dialects when compared to a pairing of a Mandarin with a non-Mandarin dialect. In contrast, a pair of non-Mandarin dialects is likely to be mutually intelligible. While historical distribution patterns as documented in *The Atlas* are far more complex, at the very least distribution vectors help explain the existence of multi-dialectal regions like the province of Jiangsu, to which two Mandarin dialect groups are native, along with the non-Mandarin dialect of Wu. In turn, co-terminous, mutually unintelligible dialects underscore an important tendency in Han dialect geography, namely that physical distance is not always commensurate with linguistic distance.

4.2.2   Chinese Linguistic Historiography

Significantly absent from *The Atlas* and *The Great Dictionary* is *Putonghua* (普通话, pǔtōnghuà). Often mistakenly referred to as Mandarin, Putonghua cannot be easily accommodated within a taxonomy of language, or indeed, be easily placed on a distribution map. Putonghua came into being in the second half of the twentieth century as part of ongoing state efforts in fostering a *lingua franca* for the nation. In terms of its phonological features, Putonghua draws largely from the Beijing Mandarin subgroup of Han dialects. In addition to its phonology, the lexis, grammar, semantics, and other formal aspects of Putonghua were to be shaped over the first decades of the People's Republic of China. Firstly identified using this label in 1955, shortly after the inaugural Constitution in 1954, Putonghua's role as national language was not recognised in the Constitution until 1982 (DeFrancis, 1984). Article 19, which remains as it was in 1982, states that "The state shall promote the common speech—putonghua—used nationwide" (National People's Congress, 1982, 2004, 2018). While Putonghua is to be promoted nationwide without infringing on the language rights of any ethnic group (Articles 4, 121 and 139), the Constitution is completely silent on dialects of the Han ethnic group. The temporal scope of the reference to "common speech" is tantalising, for until recent decades Beijing Mandarin was a distant, and to many, unintelligible dialect. As a dated estimate of Putonghua's spread, the Survey of Language Use in China found that in the period between 1998 and 2001, 84.23% of respondents learned a Han dialect as their native tongue, 13.47%, Putonghua, and 5.14%, one of the non-Han languages (Office of the Steering Group for the Survey of Language Use in China, 2006).

The formation of Putonghua out of Beijing Mandarin as the *lingua franca* of the contemporary Chinese state was much more than the straightforward adaptation of the dialect dominant in the political centre of China and the enshrinement of this modified dialect through the Constitution. Prior to the People's Republic of China, there was no *lingua franca* on a national or empire scale. The various kinds of Mandarin were at best *lingua franca* limited to some members of the political élite and residents of in regions close to the political centre of the time. The tumultuous events of the twentieth century, whether it be the collapse of the monarchy in 1911, the establishment of the Republic of China, the ensuing civil strife, and the Second Sino-Japanese War, heightened the degree of contact and contest between Han dialects and between Han and non-Han languages. These events and their consequences, themselves highly contentious subjects, continue to influence the debate over dialect choice and dialect use in China today.

The political problems of linguistic diversity in the form of Han dialects came to the fore during the Second Sino-Japanese War. Though by no means the only historical juncture in which dialects came into contact and came to contest with each other, this conflict proved to be an exemplary one. As Wang Hui (2011) was at pains to point out in his study of primary sources, the need to mobilise political support from the masses was increasingly evident as the political centre moved its way inland, especially after 1937. The absence of a *lingua franca* and persistence of mutual unintelligibility were deemed by various political leaders and their advisers to be major obstacles to be somehow overcome. Even without a *lingua franca*, well-established writing systems notionally allowed the subordination of local spoken language to written language in a hierarchical manner, much like the construction of taxonomies of dialects under a common Sinitic language. Although there was a degree of local dialect usage for the purposes of co-optation, many among the political élite opposing the Japanese invasion perceived the need for a new form of language which would transcend barriers of intelligibility while simultaneously attaching the local to the national, again in a hierarchical manner. Being closely identified with tradition, including literary tradition, written Chinese provided the basis for the prospect of linguistic unity in the quest for contemporary nationhood. As shall be seen later in the current chapter, written Chinese continues to be appealed to by leaders of post-1949 China in overcoming the political problems associated with the mutual unintelligibility of local dialects. The problems were to be transcended by the creation of a common spoken medium partly through the standardisation of a long-standing but evolving written medium. Such a common spoken medium would by definition be one in which any exclusive ties to geographical locations within the nation's boundaries needed to be severed. For the purposes of the present chapter, a critical question is policy construal of the relationship between the native dialect, rooted as it were in the land, with the created dialect, designed as it were to prevail across the nation, notwithstanding the circulation of dialects through internal migration.

4.3   State Policy and Nativism

4.3.1   Positions Within the Ideological Matrix

The formation of the contemporary Chinese state in 1949 could be regarded reductively as the culmination of colonial threats, crises of a systemic kind, as well as conflict on a domestic and regional scale. In applying such reductionism, it would be possible to make claims regarding coincidences in developmental trajectory between China and its neighbours such as Korea (Shinn, 1990), Japan (Gottlieb, 2012), and the Soviet Union (Chevalier, 2018) in respect of state policy. Again within a reductionist framework it could be argued that while the nation-states bearing these names were in their formative stages, policy on land, policy on language, and policy at large shared a reciprocal relationship with nascent nationalism. Rather than attempting to read into policy recurring patterns in political development across nation-states and identifying exceptions, the analytical approach taken in the current chapter was to situate policy simultaneously within the contrasts between the integrated and fragmented, the advanced and the backward, and also, the diverse and uniform (see Sect. 1.3.3 and Fig. 1.3). As already demonstrated analytically in the previous two chapters, the three continua making up the ideological matrix help position in relation to each other contested ideals, opinions, and values underlying state policies, thereby bringing into view paradoxes, inconsistencies, and trends among them. Earlier analyses revealed state attempts in guiding some members of the mobile population towards settlement and others towards transience in the name of citizenship (Chapter 2), and similarly, attempts in guiding some onto costly, but supported urban living, and still others onto alternative arrangements in the name of equalisation (Chapter 3). With possible contradictions between native dialect use and internal migration in mind, how would the state direct its population in respect of the *lingua franca* of Putonghua? A targeted review of existing studies below will generate a set of specific issues concerning land and language whose treatment in policy documents instruments and positioning within the ideological matrix will form the basis of analyses and reflections in the current chapter.

4.3.2 Studies of the Native Place and the Native Language

Scholarship concerning the native place in modern China has thus far been limited to historico-literary studies. According to Wang Hui (2011), the marginal status of Han dialects was countered in late Qing and early Republican nativist literature (乡土文学, xiāngtǔ wénxué), whose authors were consciously seeking to celebrate local–regional identity while residing away from their native soil in large cities. As in the mobilisation of support in the Second Sino-Japanese War, however, such literary attempts were frustrated by the absence of established styles, not to mention the ambiguous statuses of dialectal phonology and lexis. Unlike the case of the Soviet Union prior to the 1930s (Chevalier, 2018), there was no state-sponsored literary nativisation in China. Although the native place may have been marginal in literary discourse, it was certainly not devoid of political sensitivities, as compelling argued in relation to the setting of Li Shanding's novel in a rural native place within the Japanese-controlled puppet state of Manchukuo (see Duara, 2000). The native place's enormous metonymic potential had meant its appropriation in service of conflicting agendas not only in twentieth-century China but also in other national contexts as well (e.g. Applegate, 1990; Dusinberre, 2013). Thus imbued with a range of meanings, the native place was potentially subject to competing claims of familial kinship and political kinship. Radically exclusive claims regarding belonging would be tantamount to *nativism*, the notion that life could not be given full expression outside the native place, and concomitantly, the native place could not exist without distinctly local ways of living.

The rural native place had not always been accorded such significance that it could demand attachment and commitment from the populace. It was the object of disdain by some educated segments of the urban population who made up the readership of widely circulated periodicals in which anthropologist Fei Xiaotong was publishing ruminations about rural China as early as during the Second Sino-Japanese War (Fei et al., 1992). In the face of urban readers' prejudices, Fei mounted an impassioned defence of the rural populace, arguing for instance that it lacked neither the competence to gain literacy nor the practical need to do so while being rooted in the native place. Among his opinion pieces, Fei made a point of citing Tönnies' (1887/2001) distinction between *Gemeinschaft* from *Gesellschaft* to gently remind his readers that urbanites in China were in transition between the two kinds of social formations and that movement to the latter should not be based on abandonment of the former. By the middle of twentieth century then, there were already a range of ideological positions articulated with regards to nativism in public discourse.

In contrast to the politics of the native place, the broader subject of multilingualism in modern China had already received ample attention in previous studies. In particular, studies of language planning and language management policies were conducted using a variety of approaches. Bracketed in publication dates by John DeFrancis' monograph (DeFrancis, 1950) and Ji Fengyuan's essay (Ji, 2018), these studies of policy from 1949 to about 2004 underscored the state's desire of standardising writing and fashioning a *lingua franca* aligned with standardised writing for the purposes of developing a unified nation of many languages in and for the long term. For over five-and-a-half decades, policy relied on a mixture of phonocentrism and logocentrism to deal with different political challenges associated with multilingualism (Rohsenow, 2004), which apart from mutual unintelligibility of spoken languages included a dearth of educational resources, low literacy, and distinct regional identities. Through policy China was meant to be transformed from a nation of provincials into a nation with the common spoken form of Putonghua (Saillard, 2004) undergirded by a standardised written form (Zhao & Baldauf, 2008), both disseminated through formal education but crucially, without discouraging local languages such as Han dialects (Guo, 2004). Despite this apparently straightforward policy direction, the state was to remain concerned with managing the relationship between Putonghua, standardised written Chinese, and Han dialects.

4.3.3   Linkages Between Land and Language

In the period of policy period in question in the current chapter, namely 2000–2020, the Chinese state was administering a population that was not only urbanising and mobile but also multilingual in different ways and to different degrees. By the start of the policy period, China was already very different from when the 1954 Constitution was being drafted and when Putonghua was not widespread (see Sect. 4.2.2). In order to discern how the state envisioned the joint management of territory, language, and population during this period, a synoptic reading was made of policies regulating language use, language education, household registration, and provision of public services such as education. Building on the analyses from previous chapters, the synoptic reading presented below attended to the ways in which state policy linked together fractions of land to types of dialect to fractions of population. The main contrast in dialect was between Putonghua and the non-Putonghua primary Han dialect. The fractions of population in question were those able to speak or who otherwise identified with at least one non-Putonghua Han dialect. The synoptic reading did not deal directly with the languages and dialects of ethnic minorities. For the Han-speaking majority then, focus was placed on the linkages made in policy between:

1. The primary Han dialect and Putonghua
2. The place of origin and migration destination
3. The place of origin and the primary Han dialect
4. The place of origin and Putonghua
5. The migration destination and the primary Han dialect
6. The migration destination and Putonghua.

The reading was based on a collection of language planning policy documents from the years 2000 to 2020 and another of territorial and population management policy documents from the years 2011 to 2020. The first collection is introduced below in Sect. 4.1.1. From the second collection came documents analysed in Chapter 2 (see Sects. 2.4 and 2.5) and Chapter 3 (see Sects. 3.3 and 3.4). The documents in both collections were mostly regulatory in nature, although in respect of language planning the Constitution and select legislative instruments were incorporated for their topical relevance. The documents selected were mostly issued by the Central Government, with the remainder originating from the provincial authority of Jiangsu and its constituent municipal authority of Suzhou. Documents fitting these selection criteria but were not directly related to population mobility (e.g. regulation of language use in naming urban residential compounds) were excluded from analysis. Policies concerning ethnic minorities were not included given the focus upon policies targeting the Han-speaking majority.

4.4   ANALYSES

4.4.1   Language Planning Policy Documents in Question

Aside from the 1982 amendments to the Constitution, which included the brief but crucial reference to Putonghua under Article 19, the most noteworthy policy development for the next two decades was *Law of the People's Republic of China on the Standard Spoken and Written Chinese Language* (henceforth "the 2001 legislation", National People's Congress, 2000).[3] The 2001 legislation was responded to across the country by provincial authorities and their own interpretations in terms of the means of implementation within their jurisdiction (a review of the variety of responses can be found in Zhou, 2013). A policy chain— but not a chain of command necessarily—could be observed in the responses provided by provincial authorities in Jiangsu (Jiangsu People's Congress, 2006), and the municipal authorities in Suzhou charged with practical action (Language Committee of Suzhou Municipality, 2006). Apart from policy moves by law-makers, the State Language Commission, which resulted from the 1985 restructuring of the Committee for Script Reform, had been rather prolific in issuing instruments of authority since 2001, often together with other agencies of the state, ostensibly with the Ministry of Education even though the former was absorbed into the latter in 1998. Of the 24 language planning policy documents included in this study, 14 were jointly issued by the Commission and Ministry during the presidency of Xi Jinping. Overall, these policy documents were overwhelmingly concerned with language acquisition planning, language corpus planning, and language status planning (see Cooper, 1990) rather than with language usage and the attitudes of the people for whom plans were made. Centrally issued documents make

---

[3] An English translation of the 2001 legislation can be found at http://www.gov.cn/english/laws/2005-09/19/content_64906.htm.

general reference to geographical regions which may be the native places of migrants although these tended not to be identified specifically; specificity was generally left for provincial and municipal authorities to contend with, though once again without venturing into the technically and politically vexatious issues in language taxonomy and dialect geography. Migrant usage of two or more dialects and other such user phenomena were mostly not acknowledged explicitly in policy. Hence concepts such as primary or main dialect, bilingualism, and multilingualism were only implicit in policy.

4.4.2   The Han Dialect and Putonghua

Although the policy of promoting Putonghua was made clear in the Constitution since 1982, the status of Han dialects vis-à-vis Putonghua was left unspecified. According to the 2001 legislation, Putonghua was to be promoted through formal educational institutions (Article 10). This was effectively a proscription against the use of Han dialects as an educational medium. The same piece of legislation provided for the use of Han dialects under a number of putatively limited circumstances (Article 16):

1. *when State functionaries really need to use them in the performance of official duties;*
2. *where they are used in broadcasting with the approval of the broadcasting and television administration*
3. *under the State Council or of the broadcasting and television department at the provincial level;*
4. *where they are needed in traditional operas, films and TV programs and other forms of art;*
5. *where their use is really required in the publishing, teaching and research.*[4]

The 2001 legislation left open the interpretation of "real need" and "real requirement" for the use of Han dialects as opposed to Putonghua. By implication, the extent of Putonghua promotion was also unspecified. In the means-of-implementation policy document issued by the

[4] Translation in this instance provided by www.lawinfochina.com. See https://www.law infochina.com/display.aspx?id=6233&lib=law.

Province of Jiangsu, for example, levels of Putonghua proficiency were specified for occupations including those in different branches of the public service (Article 11 of Jiangsu People's Congress, 2006). Accordingly, public servants were expected to have reached the stipulated levels of Putonghua proficiency, which varied with their age and the communicative demands of their occupational roles. Notably, public servants tested for Putonghua proficiency at the age of 50 or above would have proficiency requirements waived while being encouraged to employ the *lingua franca*. The expected level of proficiency was highest for those in broadcasting, lowest for functionaries, and in between for school teachers. Those occupying the said roles while being below respective proficiency thresholds were to undergo training in Putonghua, unless the age-related waiver was applicable. Though lacking in concrete details, these stipulations were at the very least an allowance for generational differences in the efficacy of Putonghua promotion, which did not start in earnest at the earliest until the late 1950s, with tremendous variations across the nation and the province (cf. Guo, 2004).

It was unclear how consistently the 2006 policy stipulations made by the Province of Jiangsu were implemented. In the State Language Commission's own *Language Life Blue Book Series* (e.g. 2017), there were second-hand reports from 2015 and 2016 of over-zealous administrators within the province who saw it appropriate to invert the promotion of Putonghua into sanctions against the use of Han dialects by public servants in the form of demerit points. Lower down in the administrative hierarchy, public servants in Suzhou were required explicitly to conduct meetings and business with other officials in Putonghua (Bureau of Education of Suzhou Municipality, 2013), presumably even if all present were native speakers of the Wu dialect. In the same document, Putonghua proficiency was listed as a key performance indicator only for public servants in the Suzhou Bureau of Human Resources and Social Security, again presumably out of the need to interact with migrants from non-Wu dialect backgrounds. The use of the Wu dialect was not otherwise prescribed or proscribed in policies of this level. At the local level, there was a greater need for the local Han dialect than acknowledged in the 2001 legislation. In spite of various efforts to promote, even enforce, the use Putonghua, there has yet to be policy designed to replace Han dialects with Putonghua in everyday use other than in the practice of formal education.

The relative obscurity of Han dialects may have ended in recent years following a number of significant processes of symbolic construction in state policy. These processes involved the symbolic conflation of Putonghua and standard written Chinese into one unit, and furthermore, the differentiation of this unit from all other spoken and written forms used in China. All other spoken and written forms, irrespective of their geographical and historical relations with each other, or even the lack of, were represented as belonging to the alternative category (see Fig. 2.1). And into this category, both Han dialects and non-Han minority languages were placed. These symbolic processes shifted emphasis away from how languages were derived from each other towards how languages were to serve different purposes compared to each other. According to such a pragmatic logic, Putonghua and standard written Chinese were accorded privileged status in politics, public administration, media, and education. By the same functional logic, the value of all other language forms was to be found in alternative, especially cultural arenas. Hence differentiated by policy, Han dialects, along with minority languages, were the objects of preservation efforts in the *Medium to Long-term Plan for Language Reform and Development* (2012–2020) (Ministry of Education & State Language Commission, 2012). All ethnic groups including the Han majority were to benefit from these preservation efforts such as the building of corpora for Han dialects and for minority languages. The same subsumption of taxonomically unrelated languages in respect of state-sponsored preservation efforts could also be identified in *National Language Plan During the 13th Five-year Plan Period* (Ministry of Education & State Language Commission, 2016b). The clearest policy formulation was to be found in *On Implementing the Project of Preserving the Fine Traditions of China* (Central Committee of the Communist Party of China & State Council, 2017), which required Putonghua and standard written Chinese to be promoted as the national language at the same time as preserving for posterity the culture associated with Han dialects.[5] In seeking to promote Han dialects along with minority languages as the cultural heritage of the polyglot nation then, the linguistic localism of Han dialects was affirmed together with that of minority languages.

---

[5] The original statement is located in Section 10, and reads "大力推广和规范使用国家通用语言文字, 保护传承方言文化。".

4.4.3   The Place of Origin and Migration Destination

Pragmatic differentiation of land was also discernible in state policy. In respect of urban migration destinations in particular, such differentiation was especially evident in the 2014 national regulatory framework which divided cities along with points of an urban core population scale (see Sect. 2.5.2). As already indicated earlier, the framework allowed local authorities governing relatively populous cities to exercise comparatively greater selectivity over the intake of internal migrants as residents and among the latter, as permanent settlers. By all accounts, these migrants were likely to have acquired residential properties in the populous urban destinations of their choice, meaning a new place of abode apart from the place of origin.

Irrespective of the urban scale of their destination city, internal migrants unable to afford proper housing were to have their needs met in the second state project under the auspices of "the three one-hundred million people problems" (cf. Xinhua News Agency, 2014). The second state project apparently aimed to remove from the urban landscape shantytowns and urban villages by having them redeveloped *in-situ*.[6] In contrast to the beneficiaries of the first state project, these particular migrants were to have residential accommodation transformed for them so that they could maintain urban residency under governance conditions more acceptable to the state.

Less populous cities, mostly located in inland regions, were the focus of the third state project as set out in the *National New-type Urbanisation Plan (2014–2020)* (Central Committee of the Communist Party of China & State Council, 2014). Accordingly, new urban agglomerates were to be formed in the central-western region by 100 million migrants returning from their sojourn in eastern regions, or alternatively from within the central-west to locations near, but not in the immediate surrounds of, the places of origin.[7] Especially in relation to Chinese nationals whose households were registered located in the central-west, policy showed preference towards shorter but not the shortest possible distances in migration. Significantly, policies supporting the third state project did not promote a literal return to the native place *per se*, even if

---

[6] Respectively, 棚户区 (pénghùqū) and 城中村 (chéngzhōngcūn).

[7] In these respects, policy referred to 就近 (jiùjìn), which is further away from the reference point of the place of origin than 就地 (jiùdì).

the native place was invoked through such expressions as "homeward-bound migration".[8] In documents such as *Opinions Concerning the Improvement of Measures Designed for Migrant Workers* (State Council, 2014) and *Opinions on Supporting the Return of Migrant Workers and Others to Engage in Start-up Businesses* (State Council, 2015), the interpretation of "home", like the term "nation-wide" in Article 19 of the Constitution, was tantalisingly open-ended.

4.4.4 The Place of Origin, Migration Destination, and Putonghua

The place of origin was only one criterion by which the migrant population was fractionalised in support of state projects in the policy period in question. Among other socio-demographic and socio-economic attributes, employability[9] was particularly pertinent in policy linkages between land and language. High employability, often coupled with long-term urban residency, distinguished migrants deemed more suitable as prospective new citizens in urban areas from all others (State Council, 2016). Policy represented the former demographic as being more adaptive in an environment characterised by economic restructuring and market competition. This position was echoed by the Municipality of Suzhou (Municipality of Suzhou, 2016), which retained the emphasis upon employability and long-term residency, adding to these selection criteria educational qualifications (Municipality of Suzhou, 2016). According to the central government document, the selective making of citizens out of long term, highly employable urban residents was expected to have a "demonstrative effect", meaning the attraction of even more applicants of the same kind through means exemplified by points-systems (see Sect. 2.5.2).

Elsewhere, in language planning policy documents, Putonghua was held to contribute to the increase in employability among migrant workers seeking to live in urban areas (Ministry of Education & State Language Commission, 2012), evidently a different demographic to candidates primed for citizen-making in populous cities. The economic returns to migrant workers better able to master the *lingua franca* were cited as a potential of Putonghua yet to be fully exploited (Ministry of

---

[8] That is, 返乡 (fănxiāng).

[9] That is, 就业能力 (jiùyènénglì).

Education & State Language Commission, 2018). Apart from employability, Putonghua was also seen to increase the level of "refinement"[10] of Chinese nationals, in turn represented as a factor contributing to the overall capacity of the Chinese state (Ministry of Education & State Language Commission, 2012, 2016c, 2018).

Similar linkages between personal attributes to national fortunes were cast against a background of unevenness in the regional diffusion of Putonghua in *Plans for the Implementation of the Campaign to Disseminate Standard Spoken and Written Chinese Language* (Ministry of Education & State Language Commission, 2017b). In setting regional targets for the diffusion of Putonghua while employing the discourse of personal refinement, this document implied the existence of a social gradient sloping downwards from eastern regions to central regions and finally to western regions. The clarion call made by this document, which was issued to local educational authorities and local branches of the language commission, listed the grave consequences of Putonghua diffusion stagnating at the national average of 70%: poverty for many young able-bodied farmers and herders in the central-west, adverse impact on regional economic development, constraints upon the creation of a more or less affluent society across the nation, and even harm to the unity and harmony among ethnic groups. The call reached a crescendo in the following pronouncement:

> *To alleviate poverty, greater intelligence is required. Greater intelligence itself calls for uninterrupted communication.*[11]

The links between mental competence, proficiency in the lingua franca, material well-being, and statehood could not have been more explicit than in the above pronouncement. Rather more implicit was the implication that dialects and minority languages were not the way to economic prosperity and that without the ability to speak Putonghua, other forms of speech constituted a sign of mental deficit.

---

[10] That is, 素质 (sùzhì).

[11] The original read "扶贫首要扶智，扶智应先通语。".

4.4.5   The Place of Origin, Migration Destination, and the Han Dialect

The 2017 implementation plan presented parochialism as the cause of backwardness and as an obstacle to be removed in bringing about advancement. Ties to local language were associated with ties to the place of origin, rural occupation, lack of education, and all these to circuitously indicate the path forward for the central-west to eventually be urbanised by population concentration. To be sure, the call was not for greater diffusion of Putonghua to supply more labour to the eastern region, but rather for those still in the central-west, with the help of local authorities, to gain the requisite skills to engage in relatively short-distanced migration. For residents of the central-west, the place of origin may still need to be left behind in order to make urbanisation a reality in this region.

The last population language survey in China was conducted over 20 years ago. The extent and manner of Putonghua diffusion since then were only hinted at by the Ministry of Education and State Language Commission. If as they suggested diffusion rates corresponded to the rate of economic development across regions, then the social divide in the nation may partly be the divide across levels of Putonghua proficiency. The longitudinal lines by which the nation is cut into eastern, central, and western slices make rather stark the political geography of multilingualism operating in the country despite almost seven decades of language planning policy and its implementation. These lines, which are still being featured in current state policy documents like the 14th Five-year plan (National People's Congress, 2021), offer a visualisation of the realisation of teleological gradualism in *The Scientific Outlook on Development* (see Sect. 2.4.1), whereby the eastern region would lead the way in economic development, setting the standards and strategies which would eventually spread in a westerly direction. In the meantime, the migrant population could be expected to have their movements guided in part by their own command of Putonghua. Migrants fully proficient in Putonghua could accordingly stay in metropolitan urban areas. Those with almost no Putonghua could venture there too, or return home if urban life turned out to be less than ideal. Finally, for those whose grasp of Putonghua was in between, there would always be the option of moving towards townships near their rural places of household registration. Hence combined, state efforts in language planning and population management had effectively made exclusive Han dialect or minority language use in the place of origin a status mostly for those who for whatever reasons opted out of the acquisition of Putonghua.

4.5   REFLECTIONS

4.5.1   Ideological Positions in Recent Policy

In writing about language planning early in the life of the contemporary Chinese state, DeFrancis (1950) noted that China's leaders at the time were making policy towards the goal of "one state, one people, one language". As shown in the analyses above, this goal is still evident seven decades later, albeit with the additional qualifiers of regional variation and language specialisation. As expected, however, the dimension of coherence in the ideological matrix does not by itself capture all the positions taken in and by language planning policy under the presidency of Jiang Zemin, Hu Jintao, and Xi Jinping. Especially when read synoptically with population management policy, the dimension of progress comes clearly into view: Putonghua is in the service not just of the coherence of the state but also its progress by means of demographic urbanisation. Nonetheless, not all members of the Chinese nation will live in places urbanised to the same extent, speak the same language in the same way, and be governed with identical policies. In the foreseeable future at least, selectivity in state policy, a prominent sign of the diverse end of the dimension of sophistication, looks set to continue.

With reference to all three dimensions, it is almost as if recent state policy aimed at cultivating a non-nativist ethic mentioned by Hugh of St. Victor Abbey in a twelfth-century source known as *The Didascalicon* and appearing as one of the opening quotes of the current chapter. *The Didascalicon* was akin to an extended orientation guide for learners in school nested within the Parisian abbey. As noted by its English-language translator Jerome Taylor, Hugh himself made clear the autobiographical inspiration of this piece of instruction, citing experience since childhood of migration, or as it was rendered, dwelling "on foreign soil". Taylor also noted that *The Didascalicon* arose during education's own growth out of rural monasticism and towards being settled in urban, increasingly specialised centres of learning. A much narrower cline in perfection than what Hugh of St Victor envisioned is conceivable in the multilingual, urbanising, and mobile China of the twenty-first century. With reference to linkages between land and language in recent state policy, and dimensions of the ideological matrix, the person attached only to their place of origin is a backward beginner. Advanced would be the person who identifies more broadly with the nation, its territory, and its common form of speaking and writing. Exclusive attachment to the literally native place is not conducive to a future where a significant proportion of the population will be residentially mobile for their own sake and the sake of the nation. The ideal person is free to command the geolects as desired but only on the basis of learning standardised spoken and written language well. As some people will resemble the ideal person more than others, action is required to teach the national language and to lift levels of proficiency within the population. If this is not possible in the foreseeable future for whatever reason, other means are available in keeping less-than-perfect members within the national fold.

4.5.2   Nativism in Recent Policy

With regards to internal migrants of a Han dialect-speaking background, policy acknowledges nativism in various ways, and in so doing different kinds of nativism become discernible to the analyst. The aspiration for 80% of the population able to speak Putonghua by 2020 (Ministry of Education & State Language Commission, 2016a, 2016b, 2017a), a rise of 10% compared to the 2017 estimate (Ministry of Education & State Language Commission, 2017b), is at least a sign of the unavailability of Putonghua instruction, and possibly also of the unwillingness by some to learn Putonghua. Approximate as they appear, diffusion estimates have not been broken down by age or other relevant demographic characteristics in the public domain. If there is unwillingness to learn Putonghua despite seemingly undisputed economic returns to individuals (Dovi, 2019; Gao & Smyth, 2011), and if individuals are motivated by economic returns, then current policy does in effect acknowledge the kind of linguistic nativism observed in pre-1949 China (Wang, 2011). Similarly, if as some policy documents suggest that inability to speak Putonghua is a sign of the unrefined and if being unrefined is a stigma (cf. Kipnis, 2007) to be avoided, the same conclusion could also be reached concerning linguistic nativism. As in *The Didascalicon* of course, not everyone exhibits the same kinds or degrees of attachment to land, and such difference is also acknowledged implicitly in policy.

Policy is much more ambivalent about the existence of residential nativism than it is about linguistic nativism. Migrants are generally portrayed as unwilling to literally return to the rural place of origin, and as rationally trying to maximise the utility of migration by securing new citizenship in the largest metropolises for the superior opportunity structures they putatively provide. Migrants therefore need to be guided,[12] that is, incentivised in an almost pedagogical manner, so they can exercise their volition in residential relocation decisions towards the state goal of differential population distribution. So even though in a specific sense residential nativism could have been very useful in discursively framing the benefits of moves away from Beijing, Shanghai, Guangzhou, and Shenzhen, recent policy positions are tantamount to claiming that migrants are somewhere between attachment and indifference to their places of origin.

Just as importantly, recent policy has set out the futures for those who would be naturalised in the urban district hosting the transferred household registration, those who would continue to maintain a rural home and urban residence, as well as those who would return some distance towards their place of origin. Theoretically, these differentiating intentions in policy have the potential to generate new kinds of nativism, including the antithesis of attachment, and its transcendence through cosmopolitanism. For the policy context examined in this chapter at least, there seems to be no regulatory purpose served in including absolute prescriptions and proscriptions about the native place. To the contrary, leaving room for the native place to be defined variously in policy is much more conducive to statecraft than indiscriminately promoting permanent rural or urban residence. As far as official policy is concerned, it is perhaps in this ideological interstice that Han dialects are best placed, rather than as objects being planned for replacement by the planned *lingua franca* of Putonghua. If so, the obscurity of Han dialects in policy relative to their prevalence in daily life can be better accounted for than otherwise.

Furthermore, nativism could be manifest in ways not historically provided for or anticipated by policy. Among these, there is a kind of *adopted nativism* where migrants take up the predominant Han dialect of the migration destination not only passively but to the extent that fluent command could actually generate additional economic returns (Chen et al., 2014; Wei et al., 2019). There is also a kind of *portable nativism*,

---

[12] That is, 引导 (yǐndǎo).

shown among migrants living in close proximity with other migrants and locals of a linguistically distant background, where a greater sense of community was associated with reported gains to Putonghua proficiency on top of active maintenance of the primary Han dialect (Cheung, 2020). The significance of adopted nativism and portable nativism being reported thus far in only non-Mandarin speaking regions along China's coastline, among the nation's most densely populated, remains unclear.

4.5.3 Ideological Shifts

Preceding analyses and reflections have made clear the many unoccupied positions in the matrix defined by the three dimensions contrasting the integrated with the fragmented, the advanced with the backward, and finally, the diverse with the uniform. Effects and efficacy aside, policy which represents the state as fragmented, backward, and uniform or even as fragmented, backward, and diverse is inconceivable. Other parts of the matrix, such as that in which the state is portrayed as integrated, advanced, and uniform or as fragmented, advanced, and uniform seem rather implausible in relation to what is known about China today. The import of the ideological matrix employed in this chapter of course is not that being integrated, advanced, and diverse is the presumably default position for policy. Instead, it is that despite the fact that parts of individual policy documents could be placed in any part of the matrix, as a whole, policy in one domain or related domains tends to move towards the ideal over time. Paradoxically, regions of China will still by policy design experience social change at different rates and for different reasons. Expressed differently, a common tongue alone will by no means guarantee common urban membership across the Chinese nation.

REFERENCES

Applegate, C. (1990). *A nation of provincials*. University of California Press.

Baumann, T., Lee, M. W., Wurm, S. A., Australian Academy of the Humanities, & Chinese Academy of Social Sciences (Eds.). (1988). *Language Atlas of China* (First ed.). Longman Group.

Bureau of Education of Suzhou Municipality. (2013). *Work unit affiliation and responsibilities of members of the Suzhou Language Committee* (Suyuwei 2013 Number 3). http://www.zfxxgk.suzhou.gov.cn/sjjg/szsjyj/201305/t20130 506_226427.html

Central Committee of the Communist Party of China, & State Council. (2014). *National new-type urbanisation plan (2014a-2020).* The People's Press.

Central Committee of the Communist Party of China, & State Council. (2017). *On implementing the project of preserving the fine traditions of China.* http://www.gov.cn/zhengce/2017-01/25/content_5163472.htm

Chen, Z., Lu, M., & Xu, L. (2014). Returns to dialect: Identity exposure through language in the Chinese labor market. *China Economic Review, 30,* 27–43. https://doi.org/10.1016/j.chieco.2014.05.006

Cheung, P. (2020). Social Fabric in the Wujiang District of Suzhou. In B. Tang & P. Cheung (Eds.), *Suzhou in transition: Social change and development in contemporary China* (pp. 166–190). Routledge.

Chevalier, J. F. (2018). Language policy in Russia: Nation, nationalism, and language. In E. Andrews (Ed.), *Language planning in the post-communist era* (pp. 63–118). Palgrave Macmillan.

Cooper, R. L. (1990). *Language planning and social change.* Cambridge University Press.

DeFrancis, J. (1950). *Nationalism and language reform in China.* Princeton University Press.

DeFrancis, J. (1984). *The Chinese language: Fact and fantasy.* University of Hawai'i Press.

Dovi, M. S. (2019). Does higher language proficiency decrease the probability of unemployment? Evidence from China. *China Economic Review, 54,* 1–11. https://doi.org/10.1016/j.chieco.2018.09.009

Duara, P. (2000). Local worlds: The poetics and politics of the native place in modern China. *The South Atlantic Quarterly, 99*(1), 13.

Dusinberre, M. (2013). Searching for Furusato in Kaminoseki. In C. Gerteis & T. George (Eds.), *Japan since 1945* (pp. 47–65). Bloomsbury.

Fei, X., Hamilton, G. G., & Wang, Z. (1992). *From the Soil: The foundations of Chinese society.* University of California Press.

Gao, W., & Smyth, R. (2011). Economic returns to speaking 'standard Mandarin' among migrants in China's urban labour market. *Economics of Education Review, 30*(2), 342–352. https://doi.org/10.1016/j.econedurev.2010.11.002

Gottlieb, N. (2012). *Language policy in Japan: The challenge of change.* Cambridge University Press.

Guo, L. (2004). The relationship between Putonghua and Chinese dialects. In M. Zhou & H. Sun (Eds.), *Language policy in the People's Republic of China: Theory and practice since 1949* (Vol. 4, pp. 45–54). Kluwer Academic Publishers.

Ji, F. (2018). Language planning and policy in China: Unity, diversity and social control. In E. Andrews (Ed.), *Language planning in the post-communist era* (pp. 67–92). Palgrave Macmillan.

Jiangsu People's Congress. (2006). *Means of implementing the law on the standard spoken and written Chinese language in Jiangsu*. http://www.moe.gov.cn/s78/A18/yys_left/s3127/s3253/201001/t20100127_78553.html

Kipnis, A. (2007). *Neoliberalism reified: Suzhi discourse and tropes of neoliberalism in the People's Republic of China, 13*(2), 383. https://liverpool.idm.oclc.org/login?url=http://search.ebscohost.com/login.aspx?direct=true&db=edsjsr&AN=edsjsr.4622955&site=eds-live&scope=site

Kurpaska, M. (2010). *Chinese language(s): A look through the prism of the great dictionary of modern Chinese dialects*. De Gruyter Mouton.

Language Committee of Suzhou Municipality. (2006). *The division of responsibility among members in their respective work units* (Suyuwei 2013 Number 3). http://www.zfxxgk.suzhou.gov.cn/sjjg/szsjyj/201305/t20130506_226427.html

Li, R. (Ed.) (1999/2002). *The great dictionary of modern Chinese dialects*. Phoenix Education Publishing.

Ministry of Education, & State Language Commission. (2012). *Outline of the medium to long-term plan for language reform and development (2012–2020)* (Jiaoyuyong 2012 Number 1). http://old.moe.gov.cn/publicfiles/business/htmlfiles/moe/s7246/201301/146511.html

Ministry of Education, & State Language Commission. (2016a). *Notice of the issuing of departmental responsibilities in the national language plan during the 13th five-year plan period*. http://www.gov.cn/xinwen/2017-01/16/content_5160213.htm

Ministry of Education, & State Language Commission. (2016b). *Notice of the issuing of the national language plan during the 13th five-year plan period* (Jiaoyuyong 2016 Number 3). http://www.moe.edu.cn/srcsite/A18/s3127/s7072/2016b09/t20160913_281022.html

Ministry of Education, & State Language Commission. (2016c). *The state language comission's companion to the 13th five-year plan* (Jiaoyuyong 2016 Number 3). http://www.moe.edu.cn/srcsite/A18/s3127/s7072/2016c09/t20160913_281022.html

Ministry of Education, & State Language Commission. (2017a). *Notice of the issuing of the implementation plan for the promotion of national languages* (Jiaoyuyong 2017 Number 2). http://www.gov.cn/xinwen/2017a-04/01/content_5182853.htm

Ministry of Education, & State Language Commission. (2017b). *Plans for the implementation of the campaign to disseminate standard spoken and written Chinese language* (Jiaoyongyu 2017 Number 2). http://www.gov.cn/xinwen/2017b-04/01/content_5182853.htm

Ministry of Education, & State Language Commission. (2018). *Plans to win the campaign in promoting Putonghua and lifting the population out of poverty*

(2018–2020) (Jiaoyuyong 2018 Number 1). http://www.gov.cn/xinwen/ 2018-02/27/content_5269317.htm

Municipality of Suzhou. (2016). *Opinions on further promoting household registration system reform* (Sufu 2016 Number 98). http://www.szfzb.gov.cn/ 038/038001/20160906/e6acb59e-8d10-44a7-8371-b83c3ebe85ec.htm

National People's Congress. (1982). *Constitution of the People's Republic of China.* http://www.npc.gov.cn/wxzl/wxzl/2000-12/06/content_4421.htm

National People's Congress. (2000). *Law of the People's Republic of China on the standard spoken and written Chinese language* (Order of the President Number 37). http://www.gov.cn/ziliao/flfg/2005-08/31/content_27920. htm

National People's Congress. (2004). *Constitution of the People's Republic of China.* www.npc.gov.cn/zgrdw/englishnpc/Constitution/2007-11/15/cont

National People's Congress. (2018). *Constitution of the People's Republic of China.* http://www.npc.gov.cn/englishnpc/constitution2019/201911/ 1f65146fb6104dd3a2793875d19b5b29.shtml

National People's Congress. (2021). *Outline of the fourteenth five-year plan of the economy and society and targets for the year 2035 of the People's Republic of China.* http://www.gov.cn/xinwen/2021-03/13/content_5592681.htm

Office of the Steering Group for the Survey of Language Use in China. (2006). *Spoken and written language use in China.* Language and Culture Press.

Rohsenow, J. (2004). Fifty years of script and written language reform in the PRC: The genesis of the language law of 2001. In M. Zhou & H. Sun (Eds.), *Language policy in the People's Republic of China: Theory and practice since 1949* (Vol. 4, pp. 21–44). Kluwer Academic Publishers.

Saillard, C. (2004). On the promotion of Putonghua in China: How a standard language becomes a vernacular. In M. Zhou & H. Sun (Eds.), *Language policy in the People's Republic of China: Theory and practice since 1949* (Vol. 4, pp. 163–176). Kluwer Academic Publishers.

Shinn, H. K. (1990). A survey of sociolinguistic studies in Korea. *International Journal of the Sociology of Language, 1990*(82), 7. http://search.ebscohost. com.ezproxy.liv.ac.uk/login.aspx?direct=true&db=ufh&AN=10473634&site= eds-live&scope=site

State Council. (2014). *Opinions concerning the improvement of measures designed for migrant workers* (Guofa (2014) Number 40). http://www.gov.cn/zhe ngce/content/2014-09/30/content_9105.htm

State Council. (2015). *Opinions on supporting the return of migrant workers and others to engage in start-up businesses* (Guofaban 2015 Number 47). http:// www.gov.cn/zhengce/content/2015-06/21/content_9960.htm

State Council. (2016). *Notice regarding the proposal to promote the transfer of household registration of 100 million people* (Guofa (2016) Number 72). http://www.gov.cn/zhengce/content/2016-10/11/content_5117442.htm

State Language Commission (Ed.). (2017). *Study of language policies in China: 2016*. The Commercial Press.

Tönnies, F. (1887/2001). *Community and civil society* (J. Harris & M. Hollis, Trans.). Cambridge University Press.

Wang, H. (2011). *The politics of imagining Asia* (T. Huters, Ed.). Harvard University Press.

Wei, X. H., Fang, T., Jiao, Y., & Li, J. H. (2019). Language premium myth or fact: Evidence from migrant workers of Guangdong, China. *Journal of Labor Research, 40*(3), 356–386. https://doi.org/10.1007/s12122-019-09286-z

Xinhua News Agency. (2014). *Report on the work of the government*. http://www.gov.cn/guowuyuan/2014-03/14/content_2638989.htm

Xiong, Z., Zhang, Z., Huang, X., Dao, B., & Zou, J. (Eds.). (2012). *The language Atlas of China*. The Commercial Press.

Zhao, S., & Baldauf, R. B. (2008). *Planning Chinese characters*. Springer.

Zhou, Q. (2013). Language policies and regulations in China: An overview. In Y. Li & W. Li (Eds.), *The language situation in China* (Vol. 1, pp. 11–25). De Gruyter Mouton and the Commerical Press.

CHAPTER 5

Displaced Towards the Urban?

Abstract The choice of abode was a freedom guaranteed in the first Chinese constitution of 1954. The relevant article has since been removed. From that time onward, governance of residency by location has almost become synonymous with Chinese state policy. Given the above, how might the Chinese state manage the resettlement of those displaced by natural disasters? After highlighting key features of major earthquakes which struck the county of Wenchuan in 2008 and the county of Lushan in 2013, corresponding policy action is compared to discern state preference for on-site rebuilding as opposed to relocation. Despite similarities between the two natural disasters, responses to the later quake appear to be driven much more by the state's urbanisation agenda.

Keywords Housing · Natural disaster management · Lushan Earthquake · Wenchuan Earthquake

© The Author(s), under exclusive license to Springer Nature
Singapore Pte Ltd. 2022
P. Cheung, *Statecraft in Symbols*,
https://doi.org/10.1007/978-981-19-3319-6_5

Citizens of the People's Republic of China shall enjoy freedom in the choice of abode. (The Constitution of the People's Republic of China, National People's Congress, 1954)

Urbanisation is an inherent part of the process of industrialisation, the clustering of non-agricultural enterprises in towns and cities, and the concentration of rural population in towns and cities. Urbanisation is the hallmark of a modernised nation. (The New-type Urbanization Plan, Central Committee of the Communist Party of China & State Council, 2014)

5.1   ORIENTATION

Major natural disasters have the potential to become national crises. Apart from death, earthquakes and inundations bring about the loss of abode, community, and livelihood. Natural disasters highlight the state's role in meeting basic needs such as shelter, not only in the immediate aftermath but also in the longer term. Hence natural disasters, and the crises they precipitate, require official responses from the state. Furthermore, actual or perceived mismanagement of natural disasters could even threaten the state's very own existence. Despite its importance, state policy has been largely bypassed in detailed examinations of official responses to natural disasters. The current chapter zeroes in on state policy responses to the loss of abode after two large magnitude earthquakes in 2008 and 2013 whose epicentres were located in adjacent counties in the seismically active Province of Sichuan. Despite similarities in local political economy and political geography, the state had devised different resettlement policies in response to the two earthquakes, particularly in respect of the reconstitution of affected communities *in-situ*. Analyses and interpretations of these differences are offered later in the chapter, following an overview of earthquake-related national-level policies in the domain of disaster management, a description of the policy sites of Wenchuan County and Lushan County, and a selective review of site-specific research. As in earlier chapters, analyses will attend to variations in policy rhetoric, form, and function, and all three within the ideological dimensions of coherence, progress, and sophistication (see Sects. 1.3.3, 1.4.2, and 1.4.3), and be followed by reflections on their theoretical implications.

5.2 Natural Disaster Management in China

5.2.1 Making Policy for Known and Unknown Disasters

According to the National Earthquake Data Center,[1] China accounted for 1126 of the 2233 earthquakes around the world that measured 3 or more on the surface wave magnitude (M_S) scale in the years between 1998 and 2018. Of these earthquakes, 174 occurred in the Province of Sichuan. This was more than the 142 earthquakes reported from Xinjiang in the western region, 6 from Hubei in the central region, and 1 from Jiangsu in the eastern region. Partly due to the sizeable territory's vulnerability to adverse natural phenomena, disasters has had a prominent place in the nation's discursive space. Earlier, in 1997, President Jiang Zemin promulgated legislation under the rubric of *Protecting Against and Mitigating Earthquake Disasters* (National People's Congress, 1998). This piece of legislation, whose revision (National People's Congress, 2009) came into effect in the wake of the earthquake in Wenchuan County in 2008 under the presidency of Hu Jintao, provided the basis for the administrative regulations issued in the years since. The latter included notably *Regulation on the Relief of Natural Disasters* (State Council, 2010), whose own revision (State Council, 2019) was issued some years after the Lushan earthquake in 2013. The two major earthquakes in Sichuan were also bracketed by the issuing of the *National Natural Disaster Rescue and Preparedness Plan* and its most recent revision (State Council, 2016b; Xinhua News Agency, 2006). Revisions to the two documents eventually aligned them with each other in such a way which connected legislation to administration, and in turn, to implementation. Other key documents included the *National Disaster Prevention and Mitigation Plan* (State Council, 2011, 2016a), which acted as companions to corresponding five-year plans by outlining governance targets, and which were most recently consolidated into the *National Emergency Response System* (State Council, 2021) under the presidency of Xi Jinping. The state had been active and remains active in making policies not only in response to major incidents such as the two earthquakes but also in anticipating its actions given the inevitability of future disasters.

---

[1] data.earthquake.cn.

5.2.2   Contingency in Post-Quake Resettlement Policy

Although the 1998 legislation did not provide explicitly for long-term post-quake housing as a distinct aspect of recovery and reconstruction efforts, it nonetheless laid down the principle of making the county-level government an indispensable part of disaster management. Accordingly, management responsibility was assigned in most respects to "local people's governments at and above the county level",[2] a requirement in other words for administrators at this and higher level to work in concert with each other. Implicit references to long-term resettlement under Article 41 (National People's Congress, 1998) were eventually elaborated upon in Article 70 of the present, post-Wenchuan version (National People's Congress, 2009). The revision made clearer the scope of state-led reconstruction efforts, which now included housing. Administrators were also responsible for the determination of the scale and schedule of housing reconstruction in a reasonable manner, namely, "as appropriate under local circumstances", with the preservation of arable land as a priority, and most of all, based on consultation with, and participation by, local resident-farmers. Significantly, these and other qualifications of the manner of housing and other reconstruction efforts were added on top of proposed amendments only near the end of the redrafting process (cf. Xinhua News Agency, 2008). The late additions, which were eventually ratified, suggested demands not only for the clarification of state responsibilities but also of how these responsibilities would be discharged in relation to members of the populace most directly affected by damage to or loss of abode. Whereas in these respects the original legislation emphasised state provision, the present version thematised resident participation in state-led efforts. Through these legislative changes, contingency in local post-quake housing policy was to percolate down to other policy documents such as *Regulation on the Relief of Natural Disasters* (State Council, 2010, 2019) as well as those issued by local authorities. For instance, Article 19 of the *Regulation* stated that:

> *Housing reconstruction should be carried out as appropriate under local circumstances, economically and practically while ensuring compliance with disaster prevention standards.*

---

[2] That is, 县级以上地方人民政府 (xiànjí yǐshàng dìfāng rénmín zhèngfǔ).

Paradigmatically, the above changes signalled potential reinforcement of the dominant mode of commodity exchange found to operate in the policy domains of household registration (Chapter 2), public service entitlements (Chapter 3), and language use (Chapter 4). Hence recursion of policy form, function, and rhetoric within the domain of disaster management could also be expected to result from the playing out of agentive and inter-agentive relations in the local political economy and political geography. Given the allowance already made for local customisation, one would expect policy in this domain to only show a limited degree of variation in this particular respect. As shall be shown later in the current chapter, however, policy in response to the Wenchuan Earthquake of 2008 and the Lushan Earthquake in 2013 was to vary even in respect of customisation despite the proximity of the two epicentres, the timing of the incidents, and similarity in the profiles of the two locales under the jurisdiction of the same provincial authority of Sichuan. These differences in policy responses could not be fully accounted for with reference to the change of top leadership of the state or the extent of damages from the quake and aftershocks, to name two obvious candidate explanations. A more comprehensive account could only be arrived at after a synoptic reading of policy within the disaster management domain, and also in other domains as well. So that the governance of post-quake resettlement could be understood in context, the next section offers a brief comparison of the two epicentres in question, the earthquakes that became synonymous with them, and previous research on state responses to these earthquakes.

5.3   POLICY SITES

5.3.1   *Locations*

The County of Wenchuan and the County of Lushan were epicentres of the strongest quakes to have occurred in Sichuan Province since the turn of the millennium. Lying in the north and the centre of the province, respectively, Wenchuan is further away from the Sichuan Basin than Lushan. Importantly, Wenchuan is also closer than Lushan to the Longmenshan fault belt, which runs in a north-easterly direction on the western edge of the basin. Figures 5.1 and 5.2 indicate the location of the two counties in relation to the remainder of the province and of China. The provincial capital of Chengdu lies to the southeast of Wenchuan and northeast of Lushan within a radius of approximately 150 km.

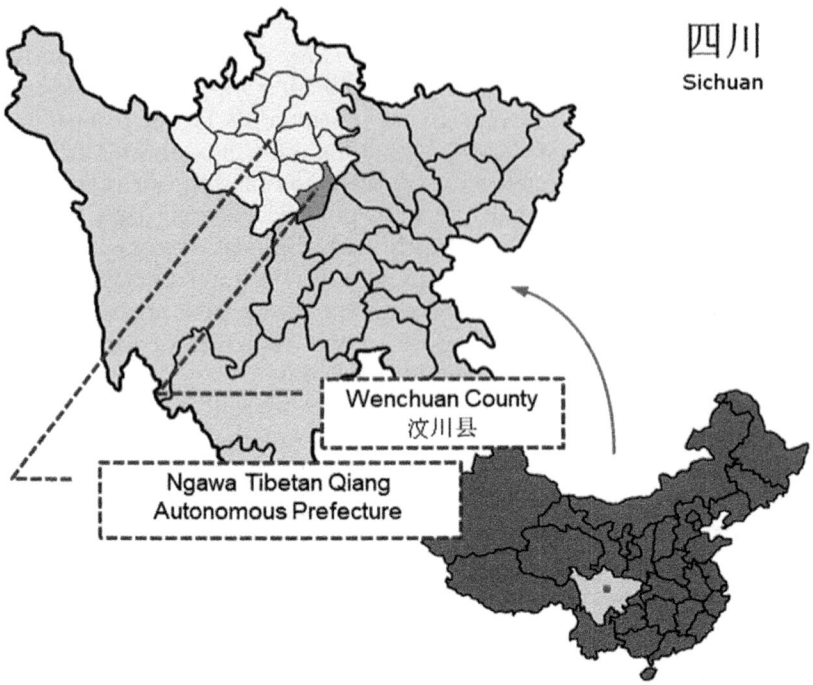

Fig. 5.1 Location of Wenchuan County, epicentre of the "5.12" earthquake in 2008 (Adapted from https://commons.wikimedia.org/w/index.php?curid=276 2216)

5.3.2   *Demography and Geography*

Pre-disaster, the two counties were on a similar scale demographically. The respective population densities were also comparable with each other, and both at levels considerably lower than for more urbanised locales in eastern China such as the former county-level city of Wujiang (see Sect. 3.3.1). Similarly, the proportion of the population engaged in agriculture, while being similar across the two counties in Sichuan, was higher than in an eastern locale such as Wujiang. Unlike Lushan, Wenchuan is an ethnically mixed jurisdiction under the respective prefecture-level authorities of Ya'an and Ngawa. The key characteristics of the two counties are summarised in Table 5.1.

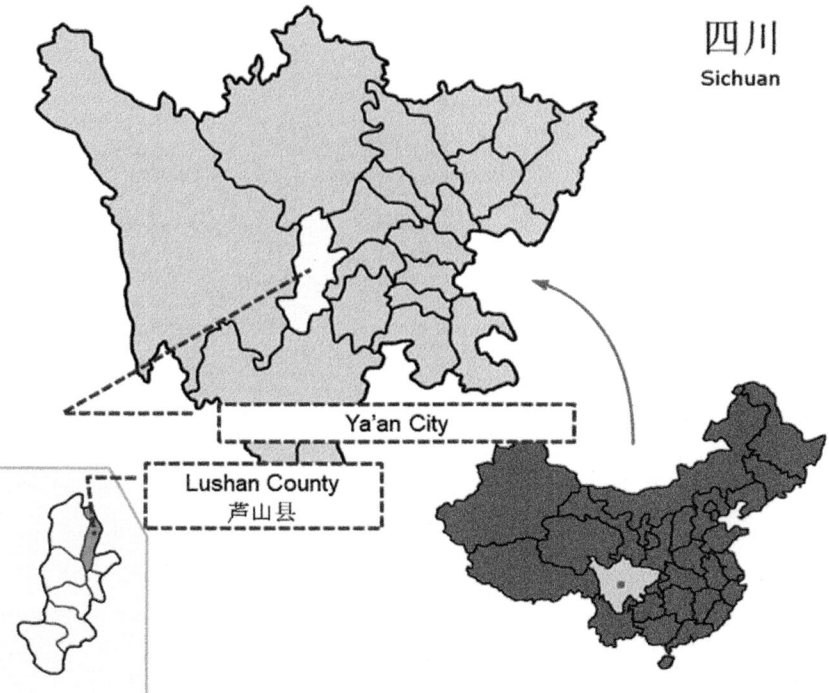

Fig. 5.2 Location of Lushan County, epicentre of the "4.20" earthquake in 2013 (Adapted from https://commons.wikimedia.org/w/index.php?curid=405 2968)

5.3.3 Quakes

Apart from being more intense, the earthquake in 2008 affected a much wider area in China than the one in 2013. Lushan was among the areas affected by the earlier quake while eventually becoming the epicentre of the later quake itself. In spite of the quantifiable differences between the two quakes, the scale of housing needs post-disaster was enormous by any account. Key figures related to the two quakes are presented in Table 5.2.

Table 5.1   Key administrative, demographic, and geographical characteristics of Wenchuan County and Lushan County, Sichuan Province

Characteristic	Wenchuan	Lushan
Administrative Rank	County under the Ngawa autonomous prefecture	County under the prefecture-level city of Ya'an
Registered Population 2007	105,000 persons	118,000 persons
Registered Population 2008	104,000 persons	119,000 persons
Farming Population 2008	64.4% of registered population	76.5% of registered population
Ethnic Composition	Ethnically mixed (Qiang, Tibetan, and Han)	Ethnically homogeneous (mostly Han)
Land Area 2007	4083 km^2	1364 km^2
Land Area 2008	4083 km^2	1166 km^2
Population Density 2007	26 persons per km^2	87 persons per km^2
Population Density 2008	25 persons per km^2	102 persons per km^2

Sources http://www.wenchuan.gov.cn/; http://www.yaan.gov.cn/; http://www.yals.gov.cn/; http://tjj.sc.gov.cn/tjnj/cs/2008/chinese/dir/chinesemenu.htm

Table 5.2   Key figures for the "5.12" earthquake in 2008 and the "4.20" earthquake in 2013

Figure	Wenchuan	Lushan
Date of Quake(s)	2008-05-12	2008-05-12, 2013-04-20
Magnitude (M$_S$)	8	7
Death toll	69,227 [in 2008]	196 [in 2013]
Total area affected in China	440,000 km^2 [in 2008]	10,706 km^2 [in 2013]
Total population affected in China	45.6 million [in 2008]	1.2 million [in 2013]
Post-quake dwellings to be repaired (projected)	1,137,500 [in 2008]	335,330 [in 2013]
Post-quake dwellings to be built (projected)	978,000 [in 2008]	187,700 [in 2013]

Sources https://www.cea.gov.cn/cea/xwzx/xydt/5583135/index.html; https://www.cea.gov.cn/cea/xwzx/xydt/5529148/index.html; https://data.earthquake.cn/; http://www.gov.cn/zhengce/content/2008-05/30/content_5718.htm; http://www.gov.cn/zhengce/content/2013-07/15/content_6528.htm; http://www.gov.cn/jrzg/2008-10/09/content_1116520.htm; http://www.gov.cn/zwgk/2013-07/15/content_2445989.htm

5.3.4 Previous Research

Comparability between the two epicentres and earthquakes attracted the attention of researchers with a variety of empirical concerns. Nonetheless, there has been no in-depth comparative study of public policy made across levels of administration pertaining to the two earthquakes. Instead, many studies focussed upon the efficacy of the emergency response in the immediate aftermath, showing for instance improvements in 2013 compared to 2008 in terms of speed and co-ordination among state and non-state agencies (e.g. Lu & Xu, 2014). Others included a focus upon recovery and reconstruction phases of disaster response, such as the perceptions of officials below the county-level in both Wenchuan and Lushan (Zhang et al., 2015). Collected through interviews conducted within 3 months of each disaster, these perceptions of officials responsible for implementation revealed from their points of view practical challenges such as the inadequate fiscal and human resources, even where the latter were meant to be provided for by policy. Another study uniquely compared recovery proposals made at the county and township levels in response to both disasters with regards to sustainability criteria (He et al., 2019). Given the national framework for disaster response presented above (see Sect. 5.2), it was not surprising that this retrospective process-tracing study should have found partial convergence between proposals between the two incidents. How these proposals, and equally importantly, policies made at higher levels diverged among themselves was not adequately addressed.

A number of other studies concerning state responses to the Wenchuan earthquake was noteworthy, such as one which attempted to relate implementation in two areas affected by the Wenchuan earthquake to satisfaction with state responses among residents (Liu et al., 2017). Although this particular study did not compare policies across the two disasters, it attended to crucial differences in implementation allowed for by the earlier set of policies in respect of the distance of rebuilt housing from the place of origin. In the sample of 300 residents drawn from the two areas in 2015 and 2016, overwhelming preference for relocation was identified. The finding, derived from victims many years after the disaster, could be considered in light of the observation by authors of an earlier policy review that resident-farmers remained deeply attached to their places of origin (Ge et al., 2010). Dissatisfaction with state responses was reported on the basis of interviews conducted between 2012 and 2013 in multiple areas affected by the Wenchuan earthquake (Sorace, 2017). This study, informed in part by reports circulated within the Communist Party of China, concluded that dissatisfied victims were nonetheless dependent upon the state for provisions as a result of layers of past policy.

5.3.5   Issues Arising

Apart from the national-level instruments of authority overviewed in Sect. 5.2, which pertained to earthquake-related and other natural disasters at large, all levels of government at or above the county-level issued specific policy responses to the 2008 and 2013 quakes. Issuing entities included not only agencies of the central government, the Province of Sichuan, but also the governments of the two counties of Wenchuan and Lushan. With the more severe and serious disaster occurring five years earlier, responses to the 2013 quake should in principle reflect the recent legacy left by responses to the 2008 quake, notably through changes to the legislative framework exemplified by the piece entitled *Protecting Against and Mitigating Earthquake Disasters*, which as mentioned above brought long-term housing to the forefront of reconstruction efforts. Policy in response to the two quakes could therefore be expected to share not only a high degree of coherence but also that of convergence with regards to their form and function. As the earthquakes occurred, respectively, at the beginning of the second term of the presidency of Hu Jintao and the beginning of the first term of the presidency of Xi Jinping, differences in rhetorical emphasis were possible, constrained though as they would have been by previously made state policy, by the recently made transition by the latter leader from the role of Vice President, and by the slowly evolving policy landscape. With respect to housing post-quake resettlement then, in what ways did policy responses differ:

1. In response to the Wenchuan earthquake in 2008 and to Lushan earthquake in 2013?
2. Across levels of administration dealing with each earthquake?
3. Between county-level authorities dealing with each earthquake?

The above questions were addressed by analysing a total of 51 policy documents in the domain of natural disaster management issued by different levels of public administration. These included 20 centrally issued documents concerning earthquakes and natural disasters at large, an additional 13 pertaining specifically to Wenchuan and 2 to Lushan. The documents analysed also included 1 issued by provincial authorities in Sichuan concerning land use in general, 4 pertaining to the Wenchuan earthquake, and 6 to the Lushan earthquake. Of the remaining documents analysed, 1 was issued by Wenchuan County and 4 by Lushan County. Highlights of analyses are shown in the following section.

5.4 ANALYSES

5.4.1 Housing Reconstruction as a Policy Gap

The doctrine of post-quake housing reconstruction "as appropriate under local circumstances" was first established in the centrally issued *Regulation on Post-Wenchuan Earthquake Rehabilitation and Reconstruction* (State Council, 2008b). This particular doctrine of locational customisation was later retro-fitted into the revision of *Law of the People's Republic of China on Protecting Against and Mitigating Earthquake Disasters* (National People's Congress, 2009), along with rhetorical elaborations on respecting the wishes of local farmer-residents (see Sect. 5.2.2 above), which were indirect references to the challenges of local rural governance arising from intricate ties between people and the land they inhabited. The administrative regulation occasioned by the Wenchuan earthquake thereby infused into this piece of legislation a degree of bureaucratic reasoning, but not entirely at the expense of technocratic reasoning. The admixture of reasoning was to recur in the broader, again centrally issued *Regulation on the Relief of Natural Disasters* (State Council, 2010, 2019), which even after recent revision has retained this doctrine.

The doctrine of locational customisation meant there was no standard policy in terms of victim resettlement across earthquake disasters nationwide, or even within areas affected by the same disaster, even if technocratic parameters such as those to do with safety and so forth remained constant. In the absence of a uniform programme of action, the sites for recovery and reconstruction were to be determined by a myriad of other policy instruments created by different levels of government. This meant a degree of unpredictably as to where victims would live, how closely to the place of origin, and at whose cost. As envisioned in some of the earliest central government policy responses to the Wenchuan earthquake (Ministry of Land Resources, 2008; State Council, 2008b) victims could only be distinguished overall between those eventually resettled *in-situ* or *ex-situ*.[3]

5.4.2   Symbolic Construction of Suitable Sites

After both quakes, the State Council issued a corresponding *Master Plan for Recovery and Reconstruction* (State Council, 2008a, 2013a).[4] Each of these master plans featured a set of measures analogous to the regulation of internal migration through the three-point urban population scale of 1978 and in its five-point extension in 2014 (see Sects. 2.4.1 and 2.5.2). Also based on the notion of limited land capacity, the post-Wenchuan master plan differentiated affected parts of national territory by means of a tripartite scheme, which effectively created zones that were "well-suited to reconstruction", "somewhat-suited to reconstruction", or "not suited to reconstruction". The latter category was referred to literally as "zones for ecological reconstruction". This master plan regarded zones as varying in the extent to which they could viably play host to development activities, in turn supposedly inversely proportional to the extent of quake-related damage. While the master plan projected 7.6, 28.9, and 63.5% of affected areas to fit the description of each category, the actual zoning of townships and towns under this scheme was to be approved by corresponding provincial authorities. At a lower level of administration, the zoning of villages would by the same reasoning be the responsibility of prefecture level or county-level authorities. The master plan requested that:

> *Towns in locations somewhat suited to reconstruction should largely seek to rebuild on-site, re-zoning land where industrial use is no longer feasible. Down-scaling of industry should be arranged accordingly. Villages should*

---

[3] In-situ: variously translated from 原地 (yuándì) and 原址 (yuánzhǐ). Ex-situ: variously translated from 易地 (yìdì), 易址 (yìzhǐ), and 异地 (yìdì). Other terms indicative of distance from the place from the place of origin, such as 就地 (jiùdì) and 就近 (jiùjìn), were also employed, albeit with even less locational precision than the above.

[4] Also referred to in studies reviewed in Sect. 5.3.5 (see Ge et al., 2010; Liu et al., 2017).

also largely seek to rebuild on-site, forming more compact communities if conditions permit.

Despite the rhetoric of locational customisation, therefore, policies in response to the Wenchuan earthquake gave priority to rebuilding on-site while studiously avoiding any prescription over displacement other than the discouragement of outbound migration *en masse*. Hence there was customisation, but mostly in relation to the options within rebuilding in or near the place of origin, again with no specifications of the distance away from it (cf. the representation of migration distance as discussed in Sect. 4.4.3). The emphasis upon rebuilding on-site was due in part to the high costs involved in relocation, which nonetheless occurred on a large scale according to some researchers (e.g. Ge et al., 2010; Liu et al., 2017; Sorace, 2014).

In the post-Lushan master plan, affected areas were differentiated by another scheme into the categories of "population-cluster zone", "agricultural development zone", "ecological conservation zone" and "hazard avoidance zone". As with the earlier quake, the zone for conservation was anticipated to occupy the largest proportion or 85.3% of affected areas in this particular master plan. By comparison, the least hazardous zones, prime sites for resettlement, were to occupy only 0.9 and 11.3% of affected areas, respectively. Unlike the other master plan, however, there were no explicit stipulation concerning zoning approval by high-level authorities and reminders to regulate housing development as appropriate under local circumstances. Although rebuilding housing on-site was by no means precluded in the second master plan, there were no signs of the "enthusiastic encouragement" found in the first master plan either. Similarly, the expression "as appropriate under local circumstances" was not employed as in the first master plan to promote the locational customisation of housing.

One of the many state agencies that contributed to the two master plans was the then Ministry of Land Resources,[5] whose overall distinction of the *in-situ* from the *ex-situ* was extant throughout the documents analysed in this part of the present study. In contrast, important as they were to the policy response after each disaster, zoning categories could only be found in master plans. These two types of spatial categorisation were quite

---

[5] Now the Ministry of Natural Resources.

literally layered on top of each other in ways that pre-determined housing outcomes by residential location at the time of the disaster. Not only did policy bring about the differential imbrication of territory and population, it did so in iterations, each with its own system of classification, and its own tendency of uneven desiccation.

5.4.3   Rhetoric of Policy Divergence

The post-Lushan master plan made reference to the need for policy to be guided by such ideological pillars as the *Scientific Outlook on Development* (see Sect. 2.4.1). The plan also asked that policy "fully reference" the "successful experiences" of rebuilding following earthquakes in locations such as Wenchuan in 2008 and Yushu[6] in 2010. While uniform policy nationwide would contradict the teleological gradualism of *The Outlook*, the master plan seemed reasonably modelled upon the one created after the 2008 earthquake. Similarities between the two master plans were only to be anticipated considering the overall features of these two particular disasters, and the fact that both quakes devastated Lushan. Much less anticipated was the apparently separate, and earlier move by the Province of Sichuan in May 2013 to request a policy review in the wake of the Lushan earthquake through "Document 37" (Province of Sichuan, 2013b). Contrary to the rhetoric in the master plan, Document 37 disclaimed the relevance and applicability of normative regulations stemming from the 2008 earthquake and asked authorities in the province not to rely on previous instruments for justifications in devising new instruments. Instead, state agencies at the provincial level and below were to review normative regulations created in response to the Wenchuan earthquake before issuing counterparts for the Lushan earthquake. This rather public act of policy intervention directed at other policy-issuing entities was especially noteworthy considering another State Council document calling for the experience of Wenchuan to be learned from in response to the Lushan earthquake (State Council, 2013b). This State Council document, dated July 2013 like the master plan, asked for such learning to be directed towards the "win–win" outcome of recovery and reconstruction on the one hand, plus economic and social development on the other.

---

[6] Yushu County, Qinghai Province.

The rhetorical suggestion that rebuilding could have been at the expense of growth was not found in the post-Wenchuan master plan.

Intervention by provincial authorities to ensure innovation aside, there was actually a considerable degree of convergence in form between policies issued in response to the two earthquakes. Other than a specific administrative regulation for Wenchuan (State Council, 2008b), unnecessary by the time of the Lushan earthquake due to a broadly applicable equivalent (State Council, 2010), policy output was comparable in form after both disasters. In accordance to instruments from higher-level authorities then, the Province of Sichuan issued "housing reconstruction proposals", respectively, for residents of rural (2008a, 2013c) and urban (2008b, 2013d) land in the constitutional sense (see Sect. 2.3.2). Aside from adding yet another layer of spatial categorisation onto policy treatment of earthquake victims, this practice connected disaster management directly to household registration and public service entitlements as policy domains. County governments, for which provincial authorities have constitutionally required oversight, in turn issued their own housing reconstruction proposals (e.g. County of Wenchuan, 2009) or means-of-implementation documents in relation to housing matters (e.g. County of Lushan, 2013a, 2013b, 2013c).

5.4.4 Provisions for Rural Housing

The province's rural housing proposal concerning Wenchuan asked for all collapsed and seriously damaged dwellings to be rebuilt within approximately 18 months, that is, by the end of 2009. In principle, rebuilding was to be carried out by farmer-residents on-site with cash subsidies varying in amount depending on household size and position in relation to the poverty line. Distance between the rebuilding site from the original site was not specified. For those whose displacement was inevitable, additional support was available in the form of housing land swap, whereby loss of rural land earmarked for housing would be compensated for in terms of relocation housing. Again, the location of new sites was not otherwise specified. Nonetheless, in policy terms, these provisions were "appropriate" by taking into account the "circumstances" arising from constraints within the system of rural land use rights operating across the nation at the time (see Wang, 2009).

In contrast, the province's proposal concerning Lushan set post-quake rebuilding of rural housing within the scope of concurrent state projects including those of urbanisation, rural development, and poverty reduction. The proposal, which contained details expected on the basis of previous practice such as cash subsidies in support of rebuilding, and the indicative time-frame of 2 years, was supplemented by a series of "dedicated plans" (Province of Sichuan, 2013a). These plans, which apart from dealing with the rebuilding of housing on rural and urban land in affected areas, also contained blueprints for the development for these areas, each with a long list of quantified targets. The considerably greater emphasis upon planning in 2013 was perhaps the reason for further specification of the Ministry of Land Resources' categories of *in-situ* and *ex-situ* rebuilding from 2008. In 2013, the dedicated plan for rural and urban housing fractionalised *in-situ* rebuilding into two types: "on-site", to be carried out on the housing land residents already held titles to at the time of the quake, and "off-site", to be carried out on another piece of rural land in the same village, notwithstanding changes to village boundaries as part of broader development. *Ex-situ* rebuilding would accordingly be carried out in villages other than the ones of resident origin. The plan also added a note of encouragement for those originally living in the core of world heritage-listed areas to relocate while forbidding new settlements in these particular locales. The latter qualifications were examples of the overlaying of zoning categories such as "ecological conservation" from the master plan onto local, disaster-specific definitions of *in-situ* and *ex-situ*.

The two proposals made by the province and related documents issued by the same level of administration also differed in respect of victim participation in the post-disaster resettlement. Revisions to the 1998 legislation in 2009 instituted the need to respect the wishes of resident-farmers through collective consultation and underscored such a need especially in locations with a concentration of members of ethnic minorities (National People's Congress, 2009). Given the timing of these legislative revisions, it was perhaps not surprising that collective consultation did not make its way to policies in response to the Wenchuan earthquake. Among those made in response to the Lushan earthquake, collective consultation was directed towards the design of housing (Province of Sichuan, 2013c), which was meant to reflect the distinctive cultural heritage of the locale (Province of Sichuan, 2013a). Despite the broad legislative basis established in 2009, therefore, collective consultation was not applied in policy terms by the province to the crucial matter of housing site selection. As already shown above, rebuilding sites were largely predetermined through several layers of territorial classification informed by a mixture of technocratic and bureaucratic reasoning. In this regard, the discourse of respecting the wishes of resident-farmers including those from minority ethnic groups was also employed in relation to natural constraints on-site selection. These constraints were referred to in the parallel expression of "respecting nature" or "respect for nature"[7] by both the central government and provincial authorities in Sichuan. Such progressive discourse implied the need for the state to work both with nature and with people living near natural hazards under the state's rule.

Indeed, post-disaster provisions for rural housing would almost always involve considerations of loss of rural land use rights occasioned by hazards and by policy responses themselves. This meant attending to highly intricate variations in such rights within and between village collectives, even as these collectives faced the prospects of relocation planned on their behalf by the state. For those compelled to relocate for reasons other than actual or potential loss of abode, the County of Lushan (2013a) detailed a series of inter-locking measures for the expropriation of rural land and compensation for land use rights to be lost in the process. The express reason for expropriation in this collection of six documents was the appropriation of relevant pieces of land within and around the county seat to accommodate basic infrastructure and public service facilities. The six documents were designed to facilitate follow-through of instruments of authority from above to effect, among other things, the nascent urbanisation of the county during the course of reconstruction. Highlights in this regard included cash bonuses, calculated daily, for early assent to relocation agreements followed by timely departure from relevant properties, all within a period of 30 days. The documents also provided for a one-off relocation allowance. Late or unwilling participants stood to lose out on these incentives according to the terms set out in these documents. The documents were clearly designed to promote rapid relocation on a collective basis in spite of different circumstances facing and unequal compensation packages awaiting individual households.

---

[7] That is, "尊重自然" (zūnzhòng zìrán).

5.4.5   Provisions for Urban Housing

Similar policy form and function could be identified in respect of housing on urban land in the constitutional sense. For the ostensible purpose of hazard reduction, the County of Wenchuan (2009) had earlier devised a policy to facilitate the rapid relocation of urban residents whose residential or commercial properties were not yet damaged in the earthquake. Although no land was to be expropriated, this piece of policy contained comparable measures as those for rural housing in Lushan (2013a). Again, cash bonuses were available to compliant and fast-acting residents in addition to compensation, which in this case was for lost property rights. Unlike the measures of Lushan, however, there was no concrete plan for making the county seat more built-up in the manner of an urban area than at pre-disaster levels.

For those who suffered damage to or loss of abode in built-up areas in the county seat, the County of Lushan (2013c) made provisions for resettlement according to whether the original place of abode was purchased, self-built, or erected by the employer. While all applicants were eligible for cash subsidies for rebuilding provided for elsewhere (Province of Sichuan, 2013d), there were different conditions attached for each category of urban residents. Cash subsidies were available to former purchasers of residential property opting to purchase subsidised housing that was yet to be built. In the same form as policies analysed above, the county of Lushan offered cash bonuses for compliant and fast-acting residents in this particular category. Measures for residents in all three categories were designed to allow them to stay within the county seat, ensuring a degree of building development commensurate with its status as a planned town, and to contribute to provincial plans for it to eventually host a resident population of 35,000 (Province of Sichuan, 2013b). Significantly, among these provincial plans, the seat of Lushan County was explicitly slated for "moderate expansion" as opposed to "large scale expansion" and "contraction", partly out of consideration of population figures pertaining to respective affected areas. The plans did not however specify the proportion of projected residents to be relocated from rural land. As of the end of 2013, the year of the second earthquake, the non-farming population for the entire county inclusive of the county seat was estimated at 37,000

(30.3%).[8] By the end of 2016, the nominal end of the three-year recovery and reconstruction period, the number of urban residents for the whole county had risen to 42,700 (38.1%). By means including policy then, housing support provided to disaster victims ensured a certain but unpublicised degree of urbanisation for Lushan and other county seats affected by the earthquake.

5.5   REFLECTIONS

In the longitudinal division of China, Sichuan belongs to the western slice, the one in which internal migration near places of origin is encouraged by region-specific urbanisation policy reinforced under the presidency of Xi Jinping (see Sect. 4.4.3). Analyses in the current chapter compared policy responses to earthquakes before and during this period in terms of provisions for post-disaster resettlement in the place of origin, and as a major alternative, away from the place of origin. For both earthquakes, what emerged was a pattern of state-led, multi-layered symbolic construction of suitable sites so location-specific that left little room for disaster victims themselves to opt for staying or moving. Policy thereby helped create the extremely parochial circumstances used to justify the limited range of options facing victims in a particular locale as well as the differences in options between locales. Although the very dense layering of symbolic classification schemes upon each other gave the state the means of closely managing large parts of territory and population, it also made the state vulnerable to the perception of inconsistency during policy implementation, as has been suggested in previous studies (e.g. Sorace, 2017).

On the other hand, responses to the 2008 and 2013 earthquakes did reveal differences in policy objectives. Among these differences, there was a subtle shift in application of the doctrine of locational customisation after the 2013 earthquake. Whereas the priority in responses post-Wenchuan was hazard reduction, post-Lushan there was the additional, even over-riding priority in local urban development. Hence apart from representing post-disaster needs differently, policies launched in 2013 had also redefined what it meant to satisfy those needs through recovery and reconstruction. In taking on some of the rhetoric, form

[8] Population figures made available in statistical yearbooks published by the Sichuan Provincial Bureau of Statistics at http://tjj.sc.gov.cn/scstjj/c105855/nj.shtml.

and function of policies in the domains of household registration and public service entitlements, post-Lushan resettlement policies sent some rural residents over short distances towards the urban direction. For some relocated residents, these policies meant exit from the rural economy and entry into the urban housing market. And it would appear that both earthquakes occasioned internal migration further afield to other regions of China (cf. Zhang et al., 2015), the type that state policy was to attempt to reverse soon afterward (see Sect. 4.4.3).

Paradigmatically, displacement of rural disaster victims towards urban areas was the replacement of exchange relations exemplified by state *provision* with those exemplified by market *participation*. Instead of only resettling members of the populace using fiscal resources, policy later attempted to employ these resources towards the end of urban development also. Not only did this require some members of the populace to be in receipt of state provision for rural housing, as before, it needed others to participate in the urban housing market, again with state support. The latter demographic, mostly state-selected and partly self-selected, were new citizens before new citizenship symbolically and publically came to be in the *New-type Urbanisation Plan*. At least in the domain of disaster management, policification of rural life resulted for some new life in urban areas, a life itself subject to the myriad of steering influences of regulations as analysed in earlier chapters. These influences had in common the preference for, and promotion of, consumptive capacity among urban residents

Whether *in-situ* or *ex-situ*, rural or urban, post-quake resettlement was largely a matter of policy and not of choice. Choice of abode, rather than being free for Chinese nationals as implied in the 1954 Constitution, became heavily conditioned by policy in population management, which in turn conditioned the state's approach to disaster management. Since the founding of the People's Republic of China, the approach to territory and population has been to avoid uniformity in policies. In these policies, symbolically created fractions of territory and population were combined and recombined recursively, thus creating tentative spaces within which similarly tentative entities could be guided to migrate. In such a view of state affairs, uniformly unconditional freedom in the choice of abode post-disaster would undermine not only established policies and institutions but also the chief state strategy of selectivity (cf. Cheung, 2021). Unlike household registration and public service entitlements, however, the increase over time in diversity in post-quake settlement policy was relatively less in overt expression and more in practical implementation. Somewhere between analogous with and duplicative of population management policies (see Table 1.1), disaster management policies were in any case developing in the direction already prescribed in the state's ideological canon. This kind of policy development was made opportune by each successive natural disaster, along with new potential for redistributing population across the territory. Indeed, the teleological gradualism of *The Outlook* was manifest in the spreading of the "win–win" discourse to responses to a subsequent earthquake in Ludian, Yunnan Province (e.g. State Council, 2014). The underlying rhetoric is perhaps best summarised by the following question: if the state could enhance prosperity while accommodating disaster victims, why not? Ideologically, therefore, natural disasters are not merely crises to be dealt with using well-proven techniques of governance, but could also lead to the reinforcement of the mandates for state projects such as urbanisation. In this specific sense, policy responses would be efficacious insofar as they promote something other than business-as-usual among state actors and societal actors alike. Perhaps it was based on this particular stance that the Province of Sichuan publicly requested that policy responses not be duplicated from the Wenchuan earthquake to Lushan earthquake.

Natural disasters do not however always provide the state with tracts of territory across which to redistribute the population in a manner conducive to its projects. Factors that influence the viability of conflating disaster response with urbanisation include the disaster's predictability and preventability, and further, the degree and duration of impact on natural resources. Whereas earthquakes are somewhat predictable but not at all preventable, inundations are quite predictable and somewhat preventable, for instance. Nonetheless, both have the potential to alter landforms and waterways, which in turn has implications for post-disaster conservation, habitation, and production. Changes in suitability in any of these respects may or may not be reversible within a foreseeable time-frame. Given the above, it is especially significant to note the breadth of coverage of natural disaster types in state policy as reviewed in the post-Wenchuan document *Hazard Reduction in China* (State Council Information Office, 2009), and less clearly specified disaster types in *The National Emergency Response System* (State Council, 2021). The more recent planning document seemed to have brought together critical incidents whose causes are assumed to be natural like earthquakes and inundations, and those that are not. Non-natural disasters were not named but were said to involve hazards such as those arising in the course of industrial production. The place of abode was mentioned as being worthy of attention, as for instance in the progressive establishment of mechanisms to ensure building safety for low-income rural residents, and the relocation of industrial chemical production facilities away from densely populated urban areas. Given all of the above, it would be of importance for future research to track policy responses in the present, that is, 14th Five-year Plan period to see how the state's urbanisation agenda might continue to shape its efforts in resettling members of the nation displaced from home by different types of incidents.

References

Central Committee of the Communist Party of China, & State Council. (2014). *National new-type urbanisation plan (2014–2020).* The People's Press.

Cheung, P. (2021). Location-specific citizenship: State visions of spatial selectivity in the cities of Beijing and Suzhou. *Territory, Politics, Governance.* https://doi.org/10.1080/21622671.2021.1982760

County of Lushan. (2013a). *Notice concerning six documents including the "Means of compensating residents for land expropriation within the county seat during the scientific reconstruction in the aftermath of the 4.20 earthquake".* http://www.yals.gov.cn/gongkai/show/20181009084800-179996-00-000.html

County of Lushan. (2013b). *Notice concerning the means of managing of subsidies for post-disaster rural housing reconstruction loans following the "4.20" earthquake.* http://www.yals.gov.cn/gongkai/show/20181009084800-180008-00-000.html

County of Lushan. (2013c). *Notice concerning three means of implementation documents including 'Purchase of relocation housing for families from built-up districts in the county seat following the "4.20" earthquake'.* http://www.yals.gov.cn/gongkai/show/20181009084800-180871-00-000.html

County of Wenchuan. (2009). *Post-disaster urban housing demolition and relocation proposal* (Trial Version) (Wenfufa 2009 Number 3). http://www.wenchuan.gov.cn/wcxrmzf/c104659/200902/023e839d64c64107b823db1b5f372e2b.shtml

Ge, Y., Gu, Y., & Deng, W. (2010). Evaluating China's national post-disaster plans: The 2008 Wenchuan earthquake's recovery and reconstruction planning. *International Journal of Disaster Risk Science, 1*(2), 17–27. https://doi.org/10.3974/j.issn.2095-0055.2010.02.003

He, L., Xie, Z., Peng, Y., Song, Y., & Dai, S. Z. (2019). How can post-disaster recovery plans be improved based on historical learning? A comparison of Wenchuan earthquake and Lushan earthquake recovery plans. *Sustainability*, *11*(17). https://doi.org/10.3390/su11174811

Liu, H., Zhang, D., Wei, Q., & Guo, Z. (2017). Comparison study on two post-earthquake rehabilitation and reconstruction modes in China. *International Journal of Disaster Risk Reduction, 23*, 109–118. https://doi.org/10.1016/j.ijdrr.2017.04.016

Lu, Y., & Xu, J. (2014). The progress of emergency response and rescue in China: A comparative analysis of Wenchuan and Lushan earthquakes. *Natural Hazards, 74*(2), 421–444. https://doi.org/10.1007/s11069-014-1191-7

Ministry of Land Resources. (2008). *Notice concerning the policy of special measures in support of post-disaster reconstruction* (Guotuzifa 2008 Number 119). http://www.gov.cn/gzdt/2008-06/13/content_1015970.htm

National People's Congress. (1954). *Constitution of the People's Republic of China.* http://www.npc.gov.cn/wxzl/wxzl/2000-12/26/content_4264.htm

National People's Congress. (1998). *Law of the People's Republic of China on protecting against and mitigating earthquake disasters* (Presidential Order Number 94). http://www.gov.cn/ziliao/flfg/2005-09/27/content_70628.htm

National People's Congress. (2009). *Law of the People's Republic of China on protecting against and mitigating earthquake disasters* (Presidential Order Number 7). https://www.cea.gov.cn/cea/zwgk/zcfg/369257/1228224/index.html

Province of Sichuan. (2008a). *Post-Wenchuan earthquake rural housing reconstruction proposal.*

Province of Sichuan. (2008b). *Post-Wenchuan earthquake urban housing reconstruction proposal* (Chuanfufa 2008 Number 35). http://www.sc.gov.cn/10462/10464/10684/13652/2009/3/4/10369745.shtml

Province of Sichuan. (2013a). *Notice concerning 11 dedicated plans made following the Lushan earthquake including the one for rural-urban housing development* (Chuafufa 2013 Number 47). https://www.sc.gov.cn/10462/10464/10684/10692/2013/7/20/10269982.shtml

Province of Sichuan. (2013b). *Notice concerning the drafting, registration and approval of regulatory documents in connection with the 4.20 strong earthquake in Lushan and the Rescinding of regulatory documents in connection with the 5.12 major earthquake in Wenchuan* (Chuafufa 2013 Number 27). http://www.sc.gov.cn/10462/10883/11066/2013/5/23/10263843.shtml

Province of Sichuan. (2013c). *Notice concerning the proposal to reconstruct rural housing following the Lushan Earthquake* (Chuafufa 2013 Number 56). https://www.sc.gov.cn/10462/10883/11066/2013/8/14/10272943.shtml

Province of Sichuan. (2013d). *Notice concerning the proposal to reconstruct urban housing following the Lushan earthquake* (Chuanfufa 2013 Number 57). https://www.sc.gov.cn/10462/10883/11066/2013/8/14/10272945.shtml

Sorace, C. P. (2014). China's vision for developing Sichuan's post-earthquake countryside: Turning unruly peasants into grateful urban citizens. *China Quarterly, 218*, 414–427.

Sorace, C. P. (2017). *Shaken authority*. Princeton University Press.

State Council. (2008a). *Notice concerning the recovery and reconstruction master plan following the Wenchuan earthquake* (Guofa 2008 Number 31). http://www.gov.cn/zhengce/content/2008-09/24/content_6121.htm

State Council. (2008b). *Regulation on the post-disaster recovery and reconstruction of Wenchuan* (Guowuyuanling Numebr 526). http://www.gov.cn/zhengce/content/2008-06/10/content_5707.htm

State Council. (2010). *Regulation on the relief of natural disasters* (Order of the State Council Number 577). http://www.gov.cn/flfg/2010-07/14/content_1661409.htm

State Council. (2011). *National disaster prevention and mitigation plan (2011–2015)* (Guofaban 2011 Number 55). http://www.gov.cn/zhengce/content/2011-12/08/content_6099.htm

State Council. (2013a). *Notice concerning the recovery and reconstruction master plan following the Lushan Earthquake* (Guofa 2013 Number 26). http://www.gov.cn/zhengce/content/2013-07/15/content_6528.htm

State Council. (2013b). *Opinions on policies in support of the post-disaster recovery and reconstruction of Lushan* (Guofa 2013 Number 28). http://www.gov.cn/zhengce/content/2013-07/19/content_5551.htm

State Council. (2014). *Notice concerning the recovery and reconstruction master plan following the Ludian Earthquake* (Guofa 2014 Number 56). http://www.gov.cn/zhengce/content/2014-11/23/content_9234.htm

State Council. (2016a). *National disaster prevention and mitigation plan (2016–2020)* (Guofaban 2016 Number 104). http://www.gov.cn/zhengce/content/2017-01/13/content_5159459.htm

State Council. (2016b). *National natural disaster rescue and preparedness plan* (Guobanhan 2016 Number 25). http://www.gov.cn/zhengce/content/2016-03/24/content_5057163.htm

State Council. (2019). *Regulation on the relief of natural disasters*. http://www.gov.cn/gongbao/content/2019/content_5468899.htm

State Council. (2021). *National emergency response system for the 14th five-year plan period* (Guofaban 2021 Number 36). http://www.gov.cn/zhengce/content/2022-02/14/content_5673424.htm

State Council Information Office. (2009). *Hazard reduction in china*. http://www.gov.cn/zhengce/2009-05/11/content_2615771.htm

Wang, W. (2009). Land use rights. In P. Ho (Ed.), *Developmental dilemmas* (pp. 55–78). Routledge.

Xinhua News Agency. (2006). *National natural disaster rescue and preparedness plan.* http://www.gov.cn/yjgl/2006-01/11/content_153952.htm

Xinhua News Agency. (2008). *Proposal to Amend Law of the People's Republic of China on protecting against and Mitigating earthquake disasters.* http://www.gov.cn/jrzg/2008-10/29/content_1134056.htm

Zhang, Q., Lu, Q. B., Hu, Y. M., & Lau, J. (2015). What constrained disaster management capacity in the township level of China? Case studies of Wenchuan and Lushan earthquakes. *Natural Hazards, 77*(3), 1915–1938. https://doi.org/10.1007/s11069-015-1683-0

CHAPTER 6

Policy and National Life

Abstract This chapter acts as the postscript for the present volume. It begins by entertaining the possibility that, after all, public policy in China might simply be words with no real significance for statecraft. With reference to major findings presented and the paradigmatic perspectives adopted, it argues that policy does provide the substance needed for governing China, however contingently. In this way, the postscript revisits the conundrum set out in the introductory chapter, adding observations based on the study, as well as posing questions arising from it. The chapter and volume conclude with brief comments about the implications of the study for the relationship between polity and policy.

Keywords Crises · Domestic policy · Lifeworld priorities · Nation-state · Systemic imperatives

© The Author(s), under exclusive license to Springer Nature
Singapore Pte Ltd. 2022
P. Cheung, *Statecraft in Symbols*,
https://doi.org/10.1007/978-981-19-3319-6_6

To dismiss China's official discourse as empty propaganda makes China and Chinese realities harder to understand, not easier. (Sorace, 2017, p. 149)

An empty institution generally arises from a compromise over sensitive political issues. It satisfies the faction that opposes its creation because it is generally ineffective; but the policy-makers striving for its establishment have at least seen their rules incorporated in the created institution—be it a new law, a state department, or the specific layout of land ownership. (Ho, 2006, pp. 11–12)

6.1   SHADOW OR SUBSTANCE?

In the preceding chapters, public policy in contemporary China was examined for its symbolic construction of territory and population, and of the actions to be taken with regards to both. Whether in respect of household registration, public service entitlements, language use, or natural disaster management, policy made prominent the parameters within which action is to be taken, not only by the state but also by the citizenry. Policies in these domains selectively promote population movements across particular parts of national territory. The corollary, despite being less salient, is no less important, namely that these policies thereby entrench the settlement of other segments of the population in defined locations within the nation. The selectivity that policy sustains is justified by geographic and demographic variations within the nation, while in turn seeking to shape the variations themselves.

Given the continental scale of the Chinese state's redistribution enterprise, one might be compelled to ask, along with some observers and researchers, questions about the true intentions of policy. By extension, questions concerning actual policy outcomes are just as tantalising. As suggested by the opening quotes of the current chapter, Chinese politics is often paired with propaganda, and Chinese policy with mere presentation. At one extreme, one could suppose that intricately designed policy to be little more than shadows of the exercise of state authority, in which case observable movements of both human and monetary capital within China would have to be accounted for with reference to another analytical object. Even if such an alternative object exists and is fully accessible, the issue would still be the explanation of any correspondence between directions discernible in state policy and empirical trends identifiable in Chinese society. At the other extreme, one could regard policy as being able to effect the substance of governance perfectly as intended by the state upon society, in which case its constant proliferation would seem inexplicably devoid of function. Clearly, neither extreme is tenable in relation to statecraft in China.

Preceding chapters have shown that Chinese state actors craft their policies in ways which may be less esoteric than reflexively assumed by some observers and researchers. From the world-historic perspective, China, like most other states, can scarcely free itself from the concurrent imperative of capital accumulation, situated as it is within the modern world-system. Despite the concurrent imperative of territorial integrity, the nation is symbolically sliced into its eastern, central, and western regions in support of a strategy of regionalisation. Accordingly, development is to spread gradually from the east to the central-west, and eventually to the far west. Even the crucial state project of urbanisation is subject to the same developmental logic. This logic is extended from the nation's geography to its demography, meaning that state policy has had to create, and continues to create, distinctions of people based on their place or places of residence. Contrary to what might be associated with a polity that is oriented towards paternalism, prescriptiveness does not on the whole characterise the state's application of policy distinctions like "new citizens". Instead, under the prevailing conditions of world capitalism, the population engages in exchanges with the state, following rules approximately established in policy and practically confirmed during implementation. Importantly, those members of the nation who do not wish to conduct exchanges for full urban residency, publicly funded education or subsided housing post-disaster can opt out, move on, and in effect help fulfil the state's redistribution agenda. There is no compulsion from state policy *per se*, not even to learn the national *lingua franca* of Putonghua. The fostering of different types of political kinship by recent policy, while being in some sense sophisticated and progressive, raises fundamental questions over what it means to belong to the Chinese nation.

When taken together with that of world history, the action-theoretic perspective makes even more salient the manner of mutual involvement of the Chinese state and Chinese society. To be sure, state and society do not interact with each other in their entirety. Just as the state creates dissimilar fractions out of national territory and national population through policy, it has done the same to itself. Thus bureaucratised, state entities are enmeshed with each other and with the citizenry over matters including but not limited to urban education, urban housing and urban residency. Instead of providing guarantees of public goods and services in urban settings in a unitary fashion, members of the citizenry make their bids for what state apparatuses determine could be made available in locales under their jurisdiction. Those most willing and able to offer monetary contributions to the local economy stand the best chance of becoming in receipt of the particular public goods and services made available in their residential locale. In their designs, policy-makers attribute purposive rationality to the citizenry even as they incorporate their own kinds of purposive rationality. Hence policy is not only an instrument of state co-optation of society but also a symbolic site for the fusion of rationality originating from lifeworld and from system. From this perspective, rule-by-policy is contingent upon the commensurability of lifeworld priorities with systemic imperatives as well as the latter's ability to influence the former. Over time, however, incommensurability could well be exacerbated by continuing symbolic fractionalisation of territory and population. Alternatively, in spite of symbolic attempts at differentiation, lifeworld priorities may remain stubbornly unchanged and unyielding to systemic imperatives. Both theoretical scenarios point to the need for ongoing empirical observations of symbolic constructions in state policy.

When systems-theory is added to the paradigmatic mix, what comes into view are the changes to Chinese state policy as a system of societal communication. Theoretically, these are changes policy makes on its own terms to itself in reaction to developments in other social systems. With the inter-penetration of system and lifeworld in mind, these developments include responses to demands made by non-state actors upon state actors as well as those made by state actors upon each other. Self-corrections to policy seem almost always incremental, if for no other reason than their being momentary outcomes of the workings of complex exchange systems of a contemporary nation-state. Limited changes to and through policy indicate much more than merely path dependency; they point once again to the recursion of geopolitical order as the culmination of recursion on national, provincial, municipal, and even smaller scales. Recursion is however a problem ideologically for any state which aspires to transformation and for members of the citizenry who hope for betterment.

6.2   VITAL SIGNS

Its utility in statecraft notwithstanding, policy is actually part of a larger problematic of nationhood. Irrespective of how ingeniously subtle its design may be, or for that matter, how conspicuously its intentions may appear, policy remains a major source of risk for the state. Risks for the state lie not simply in the numerical excess or textual intricacies of policies, and the extent of popular support, but also in the crisis latency of policy. Insofar as states participate in the capitalist world-system, it would be necessary for them to contend with the association between policies and crises. The prevailing world-system commits participants to economic growth generated on the basis of market value as it fluctuates in response to domestic, regional, and international crises. In turn, market value is derived in part from relative and scalable distinctions of the kind created by both domestic and international policy. Even though policy might be designed to avert crises, it inevitably contributes to crises, no matter how circuitously or haphazardly. Hence the juridification and policification demonstrable with regards to statecraft are not merely symptoms of malaise within any given polity, they are in fact indicative of disorder on a global scale. Solutions proposed by those who perceive such global disorder, such as Kant's *Völkerbund*, are themselves recursions of the state. Policy, as a kind of positive law, provides the symbolic substance which makes the state a tangible social formation despite the above odds. By the very same token, policy ensures the maintenance of symbolic boundaries by which one nation is delineated from all others. If there is a particular symbolic construction through policy that is set to outlast all others in the foreseeable future, it would be that of the nation-state.

REFERENCES

Ho, P. (2006). *Institutions in transition*. Oxford University Press.
Sorace, C. P. (2017). *Shaken authority*. Princeton University Press.

Index

Printed by Printforce, the Netherlands